BEHIND CLOSED DORS

Warren Beatty, Ginger Rogers, Doris Day, John Wayne, Joan Crawford, Bette Davis . . .
In this, the sequel to For Adults Only, *Diana Dors reveals the hidden secrets of all the great showbiz names.*
Scandalous, shocking, surprising — BEHIND CLOSED DORS is all these things . . .
But the most amazing thing is that it's all true . . !

Also by Diana Dors in *Star*
FOR ADULTS ONLY

BEHIND CLOSED DORS

DIANA DORS

Associate Editor: Jack Hobbs

A STAR BOOK
published by
the Paperback Division of
W.H. ALLEN & Co. Ltd

DEDICATION

To my husband Alan who once said 'If they had named the Titanic Diana Dors, it would never have sunk.'

A Star Book
Published in 1979
by the Paperback Division of
W.H. Allen & Co. Ltd
A Howard and Wyndham Company
44 Hill Street, London W1X 8LB

Copyright © Diana Dors 1979

Printed in Great Britain by Richard Clay (The Chaucer Press) Ltd,
Bungay, Suffolk.

ISBN 0 352 30335 2

Foreword

My previous journey into the literary world was greeted with such favour and flattery, that for a while I basked in the fantasy of believing myself to be quite a good writer, something I had nursed a frustrated and ambitious desire to be for years, whilst labouring as an actress. Added to this was the fact that I had written so much for my first book in the excited fervour of it all, that many of my gossipy memoirs sadly had to be held back due to lack of space, according to my publisher! So it was with some conceit I approached the typewriter ready to launch forth into my second attempt at being an authoress, thinking that with the previously written unused material, and the compliments about *For Adults Only* still ringing in my ears, it would take me no time at all to dash off another one.

To my horror I experienced what most writers do at some time in their lives, a complete block! I was also nagged by the feeling that to try and write another book on the same lines as the first, was rather like making love to someone like Warren Beatty. Not only had it been done before, but it had been done a hell of a lot better!

As the hours passed by whilst I sat and stared at a blank piece of paper waiting for inspiration to come, I wondered what had happened to me during and after the first flush of early success. Surely I could not have gone stale so quickly? There were so many experiences and stories in my mind, but then all these things would have to wait until the day when eventually I wrote my autobiography, and this was still not the time for it.

Finally, after an agonising waiting period, and with the comforting thought that my old friend Dr. Desmond Morris had written *The Naked Ape* in merely two weeks,

I began this, my second A to Z of life, and truly hope it will make enjoyable and amusing reading.

These last two adjectives are actually very important to both my reader and myself, because the one large criticism of my last book was that it was not hardhitting enough. I do not know quite how to take this even now, but I suspect that some people expected it to be an exposé shocker, a soul-searching scandalous account of show business and my life. I did try to make it clear at the time by stating in the foreword as I am doing now, that it was not my wish to write such a book, and that I merely wanted to make my readers laugh, certainly not by hurting anyone in the process.

Alas, my attemps at trying to please and entertain without causing embarrassment to anyone but myself, were not altogether applauded, and it has been pointed out to me that this time I must not be so sugary-sweet, but give the public what it wants! To the best of my ability I will endeavour to accomplish this in *Behind Closed Dors*, and make the title exactly what it suggests, writing all the things I did not dare to do before, and possibly tearing down quite a few illusions about show business, the lives led by many of its stars, and what goes on behind the scenes in ordinary life too.

Once again I will try not to hurt anyone by doing so, and where situations are possibly too 'hardhitting' (it was my publisher's description, not mine) I will write in an anonymous vein, thus giving readers who wish to be shocked, the fun of working it all out for themselves!

A is for AUTOBIOGRAPHY

'Why is it that most actresses eventually feel the need to put their life stories down in print?' wrote a cynical, weary of it all critic. He was to an extent right I suppose, although I hate to admit anything a man says is correct, leastwise a critic! But then what about the hundreds of other people who have written autobiographies? Royalty, politicians, sportsmen, soldiers and even criminals? The urge to 'tell all' is probably within most of us it seems, and there is nothing I enjoy more than a good, honest set of confessions, providing it is honest, and not a prettily packaged, softly coloured version of the truth, as often seen on the television show *This is your Life* for instance.

The difference between the personal memoirs of actresses Hildegarde Knef and Joan Collins explains my theory. Hildegarde's is well written and earthily forthright, baring her soul 'warts and all' as the saying goes, and the other an egotistical sexual romp, which Joan, whom I will be telling a story about later, has even stooped to colouring up with fabrication. Her claim to being taken for a ride by the late James Dean in his Porsche car, the one he was killed in, makes an exciting tale, but sadly, someone like myself who has been around too long really, can disprove it in two minutes, for Joan was visiting my house on the river with her boyfriend Sydney Chaplin around the time Dean was killed and did not even make her first pilgrimage to Hollywood until some time later.

If one is going to write an autobiography, then it must be the real truth, the whole truth, and nothing but the truth, and this is why, one day, I can hardly wait to write mine, for I am longing to hear what I have to say! There is no way an actress can be 'twee' about what she has done in her life, or hide her age if she is going to expose herself in print to the public, which is why I liked the philosophy of the late actress Rosalind Russell who began her autobiography by saying, 'Life is a banquet — but most suckers are starving'!

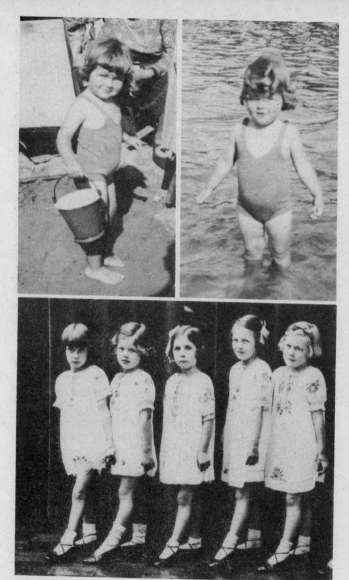

Top left. On my way. *Top right.* Taking the plunge. *Bottom.* Best foot forward.

Top. Flora Robson and myself in 'Good Time Girl.' (1947 — aged 15).
Bottom: The Rank Contract Players — but I am the only actress made to stand with the actors.

9

My best film, 'Yield to the Night'.

A is for ACTRESS

Answering this description myself, and knowing the traumas, trials and tribulations actresses have to endure, makes me more sympathetic to them than I am to *actors*, whom I will be dealing with next!

Most little girls dream of growing up and graduating from being the fairy on top of the Christmas tree, to becoming an actress or a ballet dancer perhaps, and it is from the wonderful fantasy world of childhood that actressess usually emerge full of dreams, with ambitions aimed at the stars. For a budding actress these vanities and desires are, to my way of thinking, perfectly natural. But eventually, upon wending the path through life, they are outgrown, unless of course she belongs to the small band of 'dedicated' ones who are never truly happy unless they are acting. As most actresses grow older, marriage, motherhood and responsibilities gradually take over the most important part of their lives. The greater majority then seem to find that their values and perspectives have matured beyond mere playacting. The fabulous Ingrid Bergman, an actress beyond compare and a woman who has suffered the 'slings and arrows' of fame, with all the loneliness, scandal and misery it can bring in its wake, said in an interview once that when an actress reaches forty and young starring roles are a thing of the past, the only parts left to play are character freaks or 'someone's mother'. Miss Bergman was not bemoaning the fact, she merely wished to make people understand why she was going to retire one day in a blaze of glory and not be seen shuffling around show business for the rest of her life being case in some unrewarding part here and there.

To become an actress, and even more a star, is not easy for a woman; and as the years go by her reputation, box office drawing power, and more important, the wrinkles on her face begin to make life uneasy and insecure. Without the slightest sign of distress in a business which thrives on jealousy and backbiting, she must brave the world and its gigantic microscope which reports her every move and emotion, smile at the new crop of beautiful young actresses, cope with her personal life whatever it may be . . . *and* deal with the ever-present income tax man who is always waiting to pounce, never understanding that an actress's earning powers are both short lived and erratic.

The late Joan Crawford, who was no slouch at Oscar winning, remained to the end a haunted and lonely woman; she had known great success and wealth but never found happiness personally. I made a film with her in 1966 and was amazed to find a nervous, desperately frightened woman, battling with the ravages of time and the agony of forgetting lines or possibly making a fool of herself in front of the other artistes. Some days she would struggle to perform before the camera, and after the strain of getting to the studios at four-thirty a.m. to prepare her face and hair impeccably, would sometimes run terrified from the film set to her trailer dressing-room, where the ever-present supply of vodka was swallowed down, concealed furtively by lashings of fruit juice.

Most actresses are fairly pleasant women really, although I cannot say in all honesty I am fond of them as a breed. I find their conversation and theatrical ambitions extremely boring, especially the new young hopefuls, but then this makes me sound old and jealous and I have experienced too much to be that! My immediate thought is sympathy for what they will have to go through, and always if asked by some aspiring girl or her mother what advice I would give regarding her career as an actress, I invariably say — *Don't!*

When I first embarked on my own acting career, a piece of advice I repeatedly heard was that one must develop the skin of a rhinoceros in order to survive the terrible notices which inevitably come from the critics, and the dreadful backbiting from other contemporaries in the business. Over the years I have been the victim of many scathing attacks in the press and also the object of a few catty remarks from my fellow actresses, so this warning was certainly true; but by and large, the number of bitchy ones I have had to encounter has been thankfully small.

Jealousy regarding success in the theatre after scoring a great personal triumph may cause bitchiness in some actresses, who normally would behave in a perfectly pleasant manner. A round of applause here, or an extra laugh there from the audience during any performance would transform an actress like Jill Bennett, who appeared with me in the play *Three Months Gone* at London's Duchess Theatre, from an intelligent and amusing human being to an extremely sarcastic feline! 'They are *your* kind of audience tonight,' she would hiss in the dressing room we shared together. 'Common as muck! Probably a coach party from Blackpool.' Happily not all actresses are like this. It took the late Barbara Mitchell to be the only person who brought me a huge bunch of flowers on my birthday during the rehearsal of a television show we were once doing, which was packed with men, none of whom gave the birthday, or me, a second thought.

Jealousy and 'cat clawing' in show business however, by ordinary folks' standards is pretty high, and an actress must be made of stern stuff if she is to overcome the scathing statements made by others of her profession. Standing in the wings on one occasion awaiting my call to take part in the television show *Celebrity Squares*, a young actress asked me what my 'set' question was for Bob Monkhouse's personal quiz which happens during the show in aid of charity. 'Where is the coldest place in the United Kingdom?' I quoted from the card in my hand . . . 'Noele Gordon's crutch,' came her icy retort.

A is for ACTOR

'The moment a man puts on make-up he ceases to become a real man,' said a jaded film director in Hollywood who had worked with them all. At the time he addressed this remark to me I was very young and also in love with my leading man, so I was not really convinced he was right. I

13

Top. With Vittorio Gassman in 'The Girl on the Patio'.
Bottom. My favourite actor, Alan Lake.

14

With Peter Finch

Top. Actor Michael Craig admiring himself instead of me. *Bottom.* With Jack Palance in 'Craze'.

Me and George Baker not being upstaged but upstepped by Richard Todd.

am still not totally sure to this day; certainly the man I married, actor Alan Lake, does not conform to this theory. Actors however, do appear to be like overgrown schoolboys playing at being men, at least that is how I seem to look at them now I am growing older myself and have hopefully come to terms with age and life's responsibilities. When I see Frank Sinatra or Dean Martin, shooting it out, pretending to be heroic, or John Wayne acting tough and menacing in some western, I can no longer take them seriously. Perhaps it is because I know most actors in this business too well, and so it spoils the illusion! Hollywood of course is, and always has been, full to the brim with young handsome studs from all over America eager to make their mark in films and for a woman the town is like toyland, she may have her pick.

However for the moment I am dealing with actors, not 'would be' stars, such as the car park attendants and petrol pump pullers, flexing their muscles all along the Sunset Strip hoping to be discovered. The late Humphrey Bogart when asked his opinion of the new young crop of actors in Hollywood once remarked acidly, 'All you gotta do is shout "gas" around here nowadays and they all come running.' This was perfectly true of course, but the fact that he was looking directly at Tony Curtis when he said it, put a biting edge on the statement.

Bogie, like Flynn, Mitchum, and many other of the Hollywood tough guy actors, sadly belongs to an era which is past. Whether they were real men or not, which is the subject under question here, does not really worry me, they had magic! Life was not always easy though, as other men would continually confront them in bars or public places and expect them to live up to their screen images. Poor Errol Flynn never recovered from his film *Operation Burma* where he was, according to the script, supposed to have taken the place single-handed, and this provoked many who had fought there in the actual war. Bogie too had to endure a great deal of aggravation from both men and women when he was out on the town. On one occasion in New York at the smart 'El Morocco' nightclub around 4 a.m., a woman got into a fight with him over a toy panda which she claimed Bogie had stolen from her. The case finally went to court, as in the ensuing struggle over the article in question Bogie had socked her on the nose. Under examination he was asked sombrely by the judge if he was *drunk* when the assault took place. 'Isn't everybody at four o'clock in the morning?' drawled Bogie.

Hard drinking does seem to go hand in hand with acting, particularly among the hell raisers! Whether it is due to stress or insecurity no one really knows. Like Hollywood, we have had our share of wild ones too — Robert Newton, Richard Harris, Peter Finch and Trevor Howard are merely four who spring to mind, but actors do not always have to be gigantic stars to be of the drinking and brawling character type. A dear friend of mine, the late Denis Shaw, who cornered the market in villainous roles because of his menacing appearance and downright ugly face, was barred from just about every pub and club in London during his time. The tales of Denis's adventures are almost as many as Robert Newton's; which is probably why when he died the ultimate story went round that Den-Den, as he was called, had finally arrived at the pearly gates and had been told by Saint Peter that he was barred!

Drinking is not the be all and end all of an actor's existence however. Most of them are highly nervous and intense people who actually only truly *live* when they are on stage giving a performance, for it is when they can hide behind the character they are portraying that their fears are set at rest. Disguised with heavy make-up and costume, an actor in his own mind can rant and rave, pretend to conquer the world or be anyone he wishes, but strip him of all this and he is often a shy, quiet, sometimes completely negative person.

Insincerity is another quality actors have which I personally do not like. It is never possible to know whether they are truly feeling the things they protest about or whether they are still playacting. The excellent John Neville, Shakespearian actor personified, came to my husband's dressing room one night to congratulate him

19

after his stage performance and gushed glowingly, with tears rolling down his face like October cabbages, so moved was he by it. The sincerity of it all would have been believable if Alan had not seen him casting a quick glance in the dressing table mirror halfway through to see how well he was doing!

Obviously I cannot discuss what it is like to be married to an actor unless I want a quick divorce, which will give my reader the indication that what I would say if permitted would not be very glowing, but one actor I knew actually tried to tell me solemnly that the fact that he was a Communist was because he had a very unhappy marriage! I am still trying to work that reasoning out! Beautiful raven-haired actress Patricia Medina, who laboured under the title of Mrs Richard Greene for many years, was once asked by a friend of mine what it was like being married to an actor, particularly one as good looking as Richard. Her remarks are not printable here, but the reason she gave for the actual break-up of the union was acid: 'Honey, there were just not enough mirrors in the house for both of us,' she snapped.

Some actors will do anything to get into movies. An extremely handsome English one whom I know, decided that the only way to film stardom was to lay everyone and *anyone!* He set about this immense task with enthusiasm, and blazed an exhausting trail for quite some time. Unfortunately his efforts were not seriously appreciated by all and sundry as he had very little acting talent to go with it, so he finished up playing 'bit' parts instead of 'star' parts! His reputation was of course ruined, but the death blow finally came when someone bet him that he would not dare to have an affair with a pig whilst he was on location for a film once in Yugoslavia. The poor deluded fellow, thinking this would raise his status in front of the others in the film, went ahead and did just that, only to realise eventually that he had been the victim of a hoax, and the only kind of professional status he managed to achieve, was ridicule and notoriety. So much for ambitious actors!

By and large my own opinion of actors is not very high really, the vanities which prevail amongst actresses and which I understand and make allowances for, I find loathsome in males. Ego plays a great part of course, and my sympathies are with those who felt the desire to tread the boards or become movie stars whilst labouring under physical inadequacies such as lack of height for instance. The late Alan Ladd was so short that when cast to co-star in a movie with Sophia Loren entitled *Boy on a Dolphin*, the props man was forced to dig a trench for Sophia to stand in while she was doing her love scenes with him. This cannot have done his ego a hell of a lot of good especially when he was trying to be the strong, silent hero, which is why he probably took to drink later on in his career and died an alcoholic.

England's own Richard Todd had the same problem for many years whilst he was a star at the box office, and it cannot have done his ego too much good either to know that after he had made several movies for Walt Disney, such as *Rob Roy* and *The Sword and the Rose* where he portrayed the swashbuckling hero who carried off the leading lady (in more ways than one), he became known throughout the business as 'Walt Disney's eighth dwarf'!

Over the years I have observed many actors masquerading as men, both here and in Hollywood, and it has never ceased to amuse me. I have seen Burt Reynolds manfully flexing his muscles while he sulkily lived off his wife, English actress Judy Carne. The late Richard Conte made a complete fool of himself in Las Vegas over a hooker, who led what had once been a screen tough guy around by the nose, humiliating him in public. I have heard George Peppard swear to me, hand on heart, that he had only been happy when he was a simple boy back in Ohio, and then look dumbfounded when I told him to put himself out of his misery as a film actor and go back there; and I have followed Anthony Steel from the days when he was an eager young actor at Mr Rank's Charm School, through stardom, drinking and a subsequent hysterical performance in our mutual agent's office, when he upturned the desk and threatened to throw him out of the window because of some small dispute.

To have a love affair with an actor is also a traumatic

experience as once again one never knows when they are acting or when they mean it. After swearing undying love and dragging me to a lawyer's office to ensure I applied for a divorce, from my second husband, one young Hollywood stud used to drive around town with my gold bracelet clipped to the exhaust pipe of his Porsche in order to show his feelings for me were genuine. I suppose this bit of theatricality made him think he looked like a forceful man, but he did not look very manly when my enraged husband Richard Dawson threatened to punch him up in the air, as he cowered in a corner pleading with him not to mark his beautiful face. No doubt he presented as idiotic a picture as actor Barry Sullivan did when Bette Davis's husband, non-actor William Grant Sherry, punched him over the table in the studio restaurant because of the affair *they* were having. All in all actors have not come off too well in this little piece, and I can now understand the weary words of director Burt Kennedy after an exhausting time with temperamental actor Robert Culp during the film we made together in Spain with Raquel Welch. When asked his opinion of the aforementioned Culp, Burt, who had been patience personified, replied vehemently, 'When this picture is finished, I never want to see him again on the screen . . . come to think of it, I never want to see him again on the *street!*'

A is for ARISTOCRACY

It was always my wish to have been born into the noble ranks of the great English aristocracy, not that I have a snob within me fighting to get out, but the whole mode of living which the aristocrats enjoy, or certainly used to, is my idea of heaven.

The first stately home I ever visited was that of Lord Montagu of Beaulieu, not as a sightseer, but a guest for the weekend. I marvelled at the ancient historic architecture and the old abbey alongside Palace House, the magnificent dining hall and staircase with paintings of Edward's

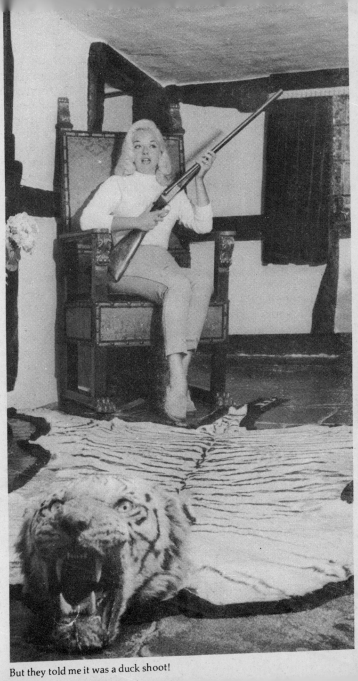

But they told me it was a duck shoot!

ancestors hanging everywhere, and longed with all my heart to be able to boast ancestry such as his. How wonderful, I mused, to sit at an enormous polished table with a log fire burning oak trees in the massive fireplace, having dinner served by a fleet of servants, and all under the indomitable gaze of one's forebears. '*That* is my great, great grandfather who lost his head when Cromwell stormed the battlements . . .' or, 'there is my great, great, great aunt who lost hers to some visiting foreign gentleman and was exiled.'

All very romantic stuff, not in the least like my own ancestors who were hard-working farmers and are buried obscurely around Somerset!

Life for the aristocracy today however is not conducted on quite such a grand scale as it used to be, although many of them still live extremely well. Peers like Montagu, Bedford and Bath have been forced to open their homes to the public and themselves live in far less stately surroundings, with perhaps the odd servant or two instead of the enormous retinue they once had.

There is of course another side to the aristocracy which the paying public never see, and I have had some interesting experiences during my adventures with the nobility.

The first titled lady I ever met, was when I hung around with the colourful Chelsea set just after the war at the tender age of sixteen. Lady Caroline Howard was a wild Bohemian character who drank heavily and was always up to something naughty in those days it seemed. She was not over-burdened with money, the family no doubt having cut her off in despair, but one night she found herself obliged to take a taxi home due to slightly inebriated circumstances. Upon arrival Lady Caroline dug deep into her handbag finding as usual that she was embarrassingly short of funds with which to pay the fare. With an aristocratic smile and oozing charm, she asked the driver outright if he would care to come in and let her work off the debt? Needing no second bidding, the astounded man abruptly switched off his meter and rushed inside!

All this would have been fine, but for the fact that some months later poor Lady Caroline discovered she was pregnant as a result of the bizarre business transaction, and this state of affairs forced her to have an abortion, which at that time cost around fifty pounds illegally, thus making the cost of her taxi ride the most expensive she ever had.

On another occasion I was sitting in a restaurant having lunch, when a man I instantly recognised, no less than the late Lord C, began berating his wife about her sexual activities during their marriage.

He was of course perfectly entitled to do this, but as the wine went down their gullets and she in turn threw accusations back, their voices grew louder and louder until the entire place heard stories about sailors enjoying her ladyship's pleasures on the floor of their stately kitchen, and all the young girls his lordship had dallied with on the floor of the library! This heated argument was of course peppered with lusty language, which made the other customers find it nearly impossible to concentrate on their food.

After these little brushes with the dignified upper classes I began hobnobbing with them in style as my career soared steadily upwards. As mentioned at the beginning of this piece, my first weekend as a guest of Lord Montagu was only slightly marred by the young Marquis of Queensbury charging at me like a bull, naked as the day he was born, when I mistakenly opened the door of his bedroom, thinking it was mine.

That memorable weekend was duly reported in the press, but as usual *I* was the one who received publicity because I dared to wear shocking pink trousers on a duck-shoot, and the press, wishing in its inimitable way to make a colourful story, added the rider that I also sported rhinestone boots! A fact quite untrue, but presenting me as the sort of person who did not know how to dress or behave whilst mixing with my social betters. I wondered what they would have thought of aristocratic behaviour if they could have witnessed and photographed my previous struggle with the young Marquis, especially as at that point we had not even been formally introduced.

An elegant dinner party which I will never forget, took place at the stately home of one of our leading peers who is related to the Queen herself. There had been a pop concert in his grounds that afternoon and I was invited for a quick personal appearance to help draw in the crowds. Later his lordship invited us all, pop singers included of course, to a private dinner with him and his wife. It was an elegant affair while it lasted, but as the night wore on and the brandy flowed, things took quite a liberal turn when I realised that his lordship was making advances to me under the table! His son and heir began rolling 'pot' at a speed of knots and passing it around, whilst one of the pop singers openly groped her ladyship at the other end of the table, an act she quite obviously enjoyed, for as her excitement grew, they both disappeared beneath the table cloth and were not seen again for some time.

Sexual romping and perversion does not only occur amongst the titled element of course. An estate agent who descended from the aristocracy (his great, great, great grandfather hid in an oak tree with Charles the Second), had no title to boast of and precious little money either, so he was forced to work in the property business to make ends meet. He did this most successfully but he was also a homosexual and one of his pet pastimes was hanging around a local army barracks when the mood overtook him, in order to try and pick up a soldier for the evening. One night his usual good fortune in this nocturnal venture went astray, and miserably he returned home, empty handed so to speak! Depressed at his failure to find a lover, he apparently performed some strange deed alone with a candle (the mind can only boggle as to what and how), and then became alarmed when the aforementioned would not move from where he had placed it. 'Whatever did you do then?' I gasped, as he related the sordid little tale years later. 'Well what could I do darling?' he replied regally. 'I had to call my family doctor.' His guests, myself included, looked aghast at the idea of the faithful old retainer arriving in the middle of the night to discover such a lurid scene, but he sailed on with the story in his casual aristocratic way. 'However did you explain yourself?' inquired an embarrassed man at the table. 'Well what else could I do?' answered the naughty culprit, 'I merely said,

"Doctor . . . I'm afraid I have been *rather* foolish"!'

All of this goes to show that if one is an aristocrat then anything may be carried off with aplomb. However it is not quite so easy to keep up with their nonchalant 'well bred' behaviour if one is a stranger to it, as a young starlet named Joan Rice was, many years ago, when she was fast becoming the new Jean Simmons in England. Joan had received a great deal of 'rags to riches' publicity due to the fact that she had been discovered whilst working as a waitress at Lyons' Corner House, but along the starry road to success she had also acquired a fiancé who came from the upper crust, with a fairly good pedigree. In hushed and awesome tones she once revealed to me that he was a true blue gentleman, from an extremely rich family, and when she went to spend weekends at his family seat it was often an embarrassing experience as she did not even know the correct knife and fork to use, despite the fact that she had obviously laid quite a few tables at Lyons' during her waitress days. I was a little sceptical about her fiancé's background, because it seemed to me he was actually descended from wealthy tradesmen, and was probably one of the 'nouveaux riche'. 'Are you sure he is an aristocrat?' I asked sympathetically, 'if he really is, you would not be embarrassed like that on visits with his family.' 'Oh yes, I *know* he is a real gentleman,' replied Joan triumphantly. 'You see whenever we are out at a restaurant having a meal, he *always* sends the wine back!'

My own favourite aristocrats were a delightful old pair named Sir Louis and Lady Stereing, both sadly passed on, but in their day a fabulously wealthy and colourful couple, whose hospitality, particularly towards show business folk, was boundless. At their beautiful home in Millionaires' Row, London, parties would be held every Sunday, and one could also see them at Cannes during the season on the fashionable terrace of the Carlton Hotel with a large table open for lunch to anyone they knew who was passing by. Elderly people who are amusing, and whose experiences of life are vast have always appealed to me, and as with Sir Louis and his wife I infinitely prefer their company to that of younger individuals.

The first time I met them was in Bournemouth, at a party after a show in which I was appearing. They were fairly elderly even then, Ethel in her early eighties, and Louis in his late seventies. Upon being introduced, Louis leaned over to me and said quite blatantly, 'You are the only girl here tonight who makes me wish I was "sixty-nine" again.' Thus commenced our friendship, and it was at one of their famous parties in London that I saw them in action for the first time.

As usual, an assembly of thirty people, some from show business, and other personages, sat at the longest dining table I have ever seen, sampling excellent cuisine amidst silver and crystal elegance, and served impeccably by a row of servants headed by the sedate butler.

The conversation was amusing and pleasant, when Sir Louis raised his glass to toast his 'bride' as he called her, miles away down at the other end. Unfortunately Lady Ethel was a little hard of hearing, and also at that precise moment growing increasingly impatient with the butler's slowness in serving the gravy, as her meat and potatoes were getting cold. 'To my Princess,' called Sir Louis gallantly, his glass raised high, and we all turned smilingly to our hostess. 'Hurry up with that fucking gravy,' came her ladyship's irritated command to the butler.

After dinner, and a fascinating evening in the library, where a magician had been engaged to entertain the guests with amazing tricks, the party began to break up. It was late and I observed Lady Sterling sitting on a very grand ornate chair in the hall, wearily saying goodnight to everyone, with the air of a queen on her throne. 'We had better be going too,' I said to Sir Louis. 'What for? The night is still young,' replied the irrepressible old rogue. 'Well your wife is looking very tired, it's time she got some sleep,' I remarked sympathetically, thinking that at her age, and with the weight of the diamond tiara perched on top of her head, she must be feeling we had all outstayed our welcome. 'Sleep,' he yelled exuberantly, 'She's not going to sleep yet. When I get her upstairs I'm going to give her one!'

B is for BLUSH

To see a 'maiden blush' is nearly a thing of the past in this day and age. There are a few who still do I imagine, and on the few occasions I have witnessed a blushing lady, quite obviously embarrassed over a certain situation, it has come as rather a refreshing surprise. So many females today are totally hardened to swearing, and open discussion on sex and the feminine anatomy, that to blush when the conversation takes a strong turn, belongs to a bygone era, long before Women's Lib or anything else.

I suppose *I* have blushed a few times in my life, although I would not say I am, or ever have been, a shrinking violet. Perhaps if I were beginning my career again, God forbid, I would certainly blush at many of the things young actresses have to do nowadays in films if they wish to get anywhere. During my reign as sex queen of the British film industry had I been asked to strip off completely or play a heavy pornographic scene, I would have refused, slightly hot around the cheeks at the suggestion! There were of course all those scenes when I was *apparently* nude, but always lurking somewhere under the foam in a bathrub or a bed was a discreetly hidden flesh-coloured bra or leotard. Would my face have been red if something had slipped, however! In essence what I am really saying is that I do not blush easily, but there was one incident in my life which did cause me to do so.

This action took place in Milan, Italy where I was appearing on an Italian television show. Accompanied by my manager I had been given a sumptuous penthouse suite, complete with spiral staircase leading up to an unbelievably glamorous bedroom which boasted a round king-sized bed with oyster silk bedspread and cushions designed for no one less than a princess. One almost felt that had it been a film set, Hedy Lamarr as 'Delilah' would have laid beautifully on it as she tempted 'Samson', played by Victor Mature.

Personally speaking I regarded it all as a wicked waste for I had no husband or lover with me, only the afore-mentioned manager whose purpose in my life was solely

The cover of 'Diana Dors in 3-D'.

business. However, I settled happily into my luxurious quarters and got on with the television show, resigning myself to life and its circumstances.

Proving my point in 'On The Double' which I made in Hollywood with Danny Kaye.

On the second day after my arrival in Milan an extremely famous Italian sex symbol star, whom I knew well, called and asked me if she could bring her latest, and secret boyfriend to my suite for a love-making session before she flew off to Hollywood. She wanted to keep the whole thing hush-hush, was distraught at the parting between them which was to follow, and obviously intended to make the most of their last hours together.

I agreed readily, adding that I would not be back until later in the evening, thus leaving the way clear for them all afternoon, and that I would place the key in a special spot, so that she would not have to reveal herself at the reception desk.

Presumably all went well, for when I returned they had gone, and so, I noted, had the oyster silk bedspread, but as the bedroom area where they had kept their tryst was now in apple pie order, I imagined the maids had probably tidied up. The following morning it was time to leave for England, and as I sat on the balcony overlooking the great cathedral, my manager walked in accompanied by a woman. He had a curious look on his face. 'You went out early,' I quipped, thinking he had picked up a bird for a few moments' pleasure before our departure — something he had been vainly attempting to do for two days. 'Careful,' he warned, 'She understands a little English, but it's not what you think, I promise.' 'Oh really,' I grinned. 'Have you brought her up here to discuss politics?' 'This lady is the hotel housekeeper,' he announced, 'And when I tell you what she *does* want to discuss, it will soon take the smile off your face.'

I could not comprehend this last statement and his general attitude seemed strange, but he proceeded to explain with various winks and private signals. 'It appears that the housekeeper is distressed over the state of your bedspread,' he said in a dignified manner. 'My bedspread?' I answered, 'Why?' 'Well it is at this precise moment with the management, because the housekeeper says it is ruined.' 'What the hell has that got to do with *me*?' I demanded. 'The er . . . friends who were here,' he tried to explain pointedly, 'they must have ripped it or something.' Guardedly I managed to convey to the woman that I did not understand what anyone was talking about, and that if the bedspread was damaged then it could not possibly be anything very serious, which seemed to appease her, for off she went, an odd smile lurking at the corners of her mouth, as though she thought I had obviously had some terrific fun in my suite.

The fact remained however, that the article had been damaged by my sx goddess friend and her lover, but I was regarded quite naturally as the culprit!

My manager was no becoming belligerent. 'What the hell, it's part of the risk any hotel takes,' he muttered. 'And at these prices they will just have to put up with it. Are you packed and ready?' I assured him I was, and so with the aid of a couple of porters we made our way down to the lobby.

I do not think either he or I were prepared for the scene which was then to follow. Standing by the ornate desk were three managers, all looking extremely angry in their frock coats, with the offending bedspread held up aloft between them for all to see, with the signs of the apparent lovemaking damage very much to the fore. Even my manager went slightly red. 'Go and get in the car,' he ordered, 'I'll sort this out.' I walked towards the swing doors but all eyes were on me, and I knew that whatever he said and did everyone in that hotel lobby believed I was to blame. A heated argument followed, some of which I could still hear as I sank gratefully into the privacy of the car outside, blushing to the roots of my bleached blonde hair.

The three managers, who all spoke perfect English, were not in agreement with him that I was not responsible, or that the money should come off the hotel insurance. A shouting match started between them which attracted a great deal of attention from all and sundry, as by now the whole affair had graduated into the street with my manager rushing to get to the car.

'Step on it driver,' he yelled at the chauffeur who was also fascinated by the entire scene, along with many passers by, for it was not every day they saw three frock-coated managers pursuing an English film star, waving a large silk bedspread above their heads, and swearing loud threats in their native tongue.

As our car sped away *my* manager, on one vain last attempt to prove his case and uphold British dignity, shouted through the window, 'It's fair wear and tear gentlemen!' A statement which sadly did not impress anyone, or help to counteract my deeply embarrassed blush.

B is for LIONEL BLAIR

I have known Lionel and his equally talented sister Joyce for more years than any of us care to remember. They are a unique pair — utterly devoted to each other, and I have always felt that if they had been around in the twenties, showbusiness would have regarded them as stars in the same way as Fred and Adele Astaire.

It is a known fact with show people that wherever one goes, be it professionally or socially, either Lionel or Joyce are bound to be there, sometimes both together. They love the theatre and regard everything connected with it as a great and unending delight, which sometimes brings forth scathing remarks from many of their jealous contemporaries.

Poor Lionel has been the victim of several wicked jokes because of his close friendship with Sammy Davis Jnr. but happily he always manages to override them. One particularly serious story went around when Sammy had been over here for some time starring in the stage show *Golden Boy*. People were apprehended with the terrible news that on his return to America, Sammy had had to undergo serious surgery. When asked in horror what the nature of the problem was, the enquirer was then told, that he had had to have the operation to get Lionel Blair off his back! This of course was nearly as acid a remark as the one made by actor Victor Maddern, after listening to actor David Lodge's tales of *his* close friendship with Peter Sellers during their RAF days and on into show business. Quipped Maddern, having heard his praise of Peter for the hundreth time, 'David Lodge is the only man I know with a fully furnished flat up Peter Sellers' arse.'

Joyce Blair is not slow either when it comes to a biting statement. When asked once what she thought of a very popular singing star's friendship rating she replied, 'I know that if I ever invite her round to my place she will be there . . . providing she has nothing better to do!'

But back to Lionel, I have appeared with him in a number of television shows, including *Celebrity Squares*, and he always amuses me with a new joke or a bit of gossip. It was to his credit that on the last show we did together he asked if I had heard about the new series he was going to do on TV with the famous cook Fanny Cradock. 'What is it entitled?' I asked, falling straight into his trap. *'Butch Casserole and the One Dance Yid'* he beamed.

34

B is for BREAKFAST

A meal I never eat unless of course it is served at an hotel, where somehow I always fancy 'the works'. Perhaps it's the luxury of not having to get it oneself. I have had some memorable breakfasts in my life, not the least one of champagne and orange juice at the exclusive George Cinq Hotel in Paris. It was served by a handsome, Oscar-winning actor with whom I was having a big romance at the time, but if that was the best, then the worst, and certainly the most disappointing, was at the home of one of the most eminent peers in the country. A group of friends and I had been invited there for the weekend and, being as fond of food as I am, I imagined breakfast in the stately dining room would be nothing less than the kind in which the Edwardians delighted, sideboards groaning with silver dishes full of every kind of mouthwatering concoction from kedgeree, bacon, eggs, and sausages, to cereals, fruit, toast, doughnuts and six kinds of jam and marmalade. On the morning after our arrival I was awakened by a stately butler who drew back the curtains of the four poster I had slumbered in and stood to attention with a small glass of orange juice on a gold saucer. I thanked him and sat there sipping it after he had gone out, working up a marvellous appetite for the goodies which I hoped were to come. The only inconvenience was having to get up and dress to have it, as it was extremely cold in the stately home, but then I reasoned that this was the way the gentry always behaved, so I would have to take the rough with the smooth.

Having done this, I made my way to the dining room expecting to be greeted by His Lordship from behind an enormous pot of coffee with all the food around him. Instead, I perceived my host at the head of an enormous polished dining table, hastily spooning up a quick bowl of Weetabix, and rushing off with apologies about having to see to some shooting arrangements. None of my friends had appeared as yet, and it was obvious Her Ladyship was doing the sensible thing and staying in bed. I looked around — not a vestige of food was on the sideboard, and the portraits of his ancestors stared down at me with disapproval. After what seemed an interminable wait the butler entered and asked me how long I liked my eggs boiled, I warmed at once thinking that now at last a great trolley with hot plates was going to be wheeled in and everything would be lovely. As I was in the middle of telling him that 'four minutes would be fine', one of my friends entered, was asked the same question regarding boiled eggs, and we then sat and waited. Finally, to our dismay, no trolley appeared, but the butler did, looking as though he was at the start of a marathon race with a spoon containing an egg in each hand which he deposited for both of us, and then rushed off again for two more. I don't really remember much of what happened after that, I was too disappointed to speak, but I *think* a cup of coffee was brought and I then decided to go back to bed, figuring that if *that* had been an aristocratic breakfast, I was better off with my electric toaster at home!

C is for CATHOLICS

Until I became converted to Catholicism I was very much against Catholics, for in my ignorance, and having suffered bitter experience at their hands when first in Hollywood in 1956, I felt they were a sanctimonious lot who preached gloom, practised 'confessing' their sins, but never actually did anything about putting them right.

Since those ill-informed days I have learned a great deal, and although I am happy in my new found religion, I am pleased that I am a convert instead of being, what is in my eyes, a born brainwashed Catholic!

No one is perfect, and where there are good Catholics there are also bad. The Women's Catholic Guild of America for instance, who see fit to crucify anyone who transgresses in their opinion; the treatment I received from them at a time when I needed help rather than criticism, made me very indignant towards Catholics in those far off days in Hollywood. Another experience of Catholicism was

Lionel Jeffries and I on the set of 'Mrs Gibbon's Boys'.

sharing the unhappiness of a relative, married to a Catholic girl, who had once been forced to make a decision about whether she should die in childbirth, in order to save the baby, according to the dictates of the Catholic Church. Added to this there was a time when I had had a brief love affair with a Catholic, who considered it so sinful to make love to me, that each time he did so, he would run off and make a full confession to his priest.

As I have already said, no one is perfect, therefore it is not up to me to judge, but often in my own church, I see one self-righteous hypocrite who is an alcoholic, and who makes life unbearable for his wife and children with violence and abuse during the week, helping the priests perform the Holy Communion on Sundays, passing the bread up on the altar, and looking pious and saintly, as though butter would not melt in his Christian mouth! At the other end of the scale, another member of our local congregation was frowned on very strictly for speaking his mind with regard to the work and money organised by the church in aid of missionaries and natives in Africa. Said he glibly one day, 'The one thing wrong about taking religion to the natives, is that it teaches them to say "Grace" before they eat you!'

When my husband Alan and I were received into the Catholic Church we asked our two good friends actor Lionel Jeffries and his wife to be our godparents. I had often been involved in heated arguments over the years with Lionel on the subject of religion and the Pope, but whatever was said he always maintained a wonderful sense of humour about the subject, which I feel is very important. Like comedian Dave Allen I think it is healthy to laugh about everything, including much that is wrong with many kinds of religious faiths.

On the day we were received, we knelt solemnly before the priest whilst he baptised and gave us Holy Communion. To my surprised delight the priest gently asked if we would like to take our marriage vows again, to which we both readily agreed, as we had been married originally in a registry office and always wished to have a church ceremony. During this next ritual my emotions got the better of me and I burst into tears, unable to even repeat the words at all, but the priest wiped away the tears with a lock of my hair and we proceeded. Eventually it was over and we knelt there alone for a while, quietly meditating, and glorying in our new found faith.

The priest had left the altar for only a few minutes, when suddenly I felt a hand on my shoulder, and turning, found that it was Lionel who had risen from his seat and walked up to us. 'Well,' he growled, in the voice which has become famous in comedy roles, such as the prison warder in *Two Way Stretch*, 'You've had the baptism, Communion, Confirmation and the Wedding . . . you may as well do the whole lot and have the *Burial* Service!'

C is for CATS

I am an animal lover, not obsessively so, but cats in particular are my favourites. I have known many in my life, and come to understand their behaviour, respect their attitudes, and admire their love of comfort and luxury.

Over the years several Siamese who all had individual characters have owned me. One fellow worked out the way to open any closed doors in my house, by jumping up on to the handle, swinging there, and pulling it down, thus getting in and out whenever he wanted. In those days I had a Boxer dog too, and although he would have been perfectly able to do the job, his brain was not in the same class as the cat's, so he simply sat and waited for the door-opening ceremony to be done on his behalf. Another Siamese I owned was so hellbent on committing suicide that we nicknamed her 'Suicidal Sue'. Having tried every trick in the book to bring her comfortable life to an end, she eventually decided to run off and live with the barman of a local hotel, who thought she was a stray and gave her refuge!

One Siamese named Juliet, after the Shakespearian herione, lasted very well until I made the mistake of transporting her to my new home in Hollywood. I have heard of girls 'going Hollywood' and letting success go to their heads, but never a cat! The last time I saw her, she was lying behind my cocktail bar, and then she disappeared, like most starlets in that town.

James Mason and his wife Pamela were so obsessed with cats when they moved to America, that all their seventeen felines went with them. To this day Pamela, who now lives in the same house alone, has still got, at the last count, seventeen or eighteen, depending on whether one or two strays have joined the household! Pam cannot resist cats, she once bought a house in Las Vegas for weekend visits, and outside the Desert Inn Hotel found a cat utterly 'destitute and pregnant', to use her own words. The lucky animal now lives in complete luxury. At the time of writing I have two Siamese, Sarah-Jane, which is a ridiculous name to give a cat, and a beautiful aristocrat

Left. With Juliet before Hollywood went to her head. *Right.* Cat fight — teaching Honor Blackman how to do it in 'Diamond City'.

called Dilly. Now I must first explain that this is merely an abbreviation of his original name, which was Dillinger, after the American gangster. I had bought him as a birthday present for composer Lionel Bart, but Dilly was so appealing as a tiny kitten, that I could not resist keeping him myself, and gave Lionel a cigar box instead! The name Dillinger was intended for an aggressive cat, which I thought he might be, but as time went on it became clear that he was a lover, not a fighter, and far from being aggressive, behaved like a complete coward, when it came to punch-ups with enemy cats. I stress the tolerance and patient character of Dilly, for it bears out the incredible way he has acted since the arrival of my youngest son Jason, who worships him, but has in the past put the poor chap through the most harrowing ordeals which no self-respecting cat should be asked to endure. There is however a bond between the two which cannot be broken, and when Jason is away Dilly is downright miserable.

Siamese do not suffer fools gladly, and have been known to be savage at times, but this tolerant cat's first encounter with Jason came one day when the nurse was off, and I was doing my best to cope with a two-year-old. Perhaps it was because during his babyhood, Jason was forced to contend with Dilly stealing his dummy, bonnet, and cuddly toys, or jealously leaping between he and I when I was trying to change his nappy. I do not know which it was, but whatever went on in Jason's mind that day, he truly got his revenge.

On finding Jason missing, I went in search of him and found my bedroom door closed. An ominous silence came from inside as I called his name, and it was then that I made my horrifying discovery. Dilly who had been having a relaxed sleep in the bathroom, was roused from his slumbers and given the full beauty treatment, or so Jason thought, for as I arrived on the scene, *there* was the unfortunate cat covered in bright red nail polish from head to toe, just having the finishing touches painted under his tail. I stood there helplessly, not knowing what to do, and finally called the vet for advice.

'Try and stop the cat licking itself, and give it a bath,' said a rather haughty lady at the other end.

'Are you kidding,' I yelled. 'Have you ever tried to bath a cat? It would fight like a tiger.'

'Well, hold on and we'll send help,' she answered.

When the vet arrived to collect the poor animal, the sight astonished even *him*. Great globs of red paint were stuck all over Dilly's fur, and he announced that they would probably have to use an anaesthetic. Such was the peaceful nature of Dilly however, when brought home later in the day, I was told that he had behaved with such dignity and restraint they had not had to use it.

Some time after this, while desperately trying to teach my son to become potty trained, or even go to the toilet, Jason decided that if he had to use that method then so must Dilly, and one dreadful day, without my being aware of it, the cat was ceremoniously carried to the toilet, placed head-first down the bowl and flushed. Any other cat would have scratched the little terror to pieces, but daffy

41

Dilly came up soaking wet, purring, and that night yowled to be let into Jason's bedroom. It was then I gave up my protective defence of him, deciding he obviously liked it all, and was probably a masochist too!

These days things are more peaceful between Jason and his friend, but there was one last occasion a year or two ago when he thought it was time Dilly should be smartened up a bit as his grandparents were arriving for a holiday. Without a word the cat was taken to the bathroom and placed on a stool, a cloth tied 'barber-shop style' around his neck, and from there on Jason proceeded to lather his face with my husband's shaving brush and trim his whiskers.

Looking back over my cat acquaintances, I can recall one woman who had a Siamese named 'Poncey-boy'. This was an odd name, but then who am I to judge other people's choices? The difficulty was that amongst her set of friends were quite a few gigolos, and whenever 'Poncey-boy' was called at least two men would leap to their feet.

My last word on the subject of the cats I have known or owned, is to do with breeding. I was once given a brother and sister, both Siamese, who literally from their kitten days, began trying to fornicate with each other at every opportunity. Against my good judgement, I was persuaded not to have them neutered as I had done with others in the past, but let them breed, and thought in all honesty that with their fine pedigrees I might be able to fetch a handsome price for their offspring. Eventually Delilah, for that was the female's name, appeared to be expecting and I happily mulled over how many she would produce, actually promising various owners-to-be their kittens in advance, and mentally totting up how much the entire litter would net me.

Alas it was not to be so easy, for whilst Delilah had dallied, and indeed made passionate love to her brother, she appeared to have been cornered and raped in the barn, by a wild black cat, who limped and had one eye! He had no doubt enjoyed himself thoroughly, but the result was six jet black kittens — and not an aristocratic Siamese in sight.

C is for JOAN COLLINS

I have known Joan, and her equally famous sister Jackie, since we appeared in a film together way back in 1951, when she was eighteen and I was nineteen. Joan was a beautiful girl even then, and after the film finished her star began to ascend and contracts were dangled under her nose at every twist and turn. One evening I had been asked to go along to a charity-organised theatrical première to sell programmes. The car which picked me up then went to collect Joan too. I had not seen her since the end of our film, and while I waited outside with my first husband, Dennis Hamilton, I wondered if she had changed much. Eventually after a long time she appeared with her mother in tow, and climbed into the car, in an obviously angry mood. She had had some sort of an accident with a bottle of nail varnish which made her late. Far from apologising for keeping us waiting, she proceeded to seethe and grumble about it, even blaming her unfortunate mother for the accident. When the poor woman tried to remonstrate with her, she got very short shrift from her daughter who snapped, 'Don't sit near my dress, you're creasing it'.

Dennis and I sat there rather upset by this show of behaviour. She was not the same girl I had worked with, and she seemed to have become extremely spoilt, which is understandable when one is young and successful.

After the evening was over, Dennis decided that she ought to be taken down a peg or two, and hit upon a plan. His first move was to telephone Joan, pretending to be a cinema manager in some outer suburb of London, and invite her to a premiere which was being held there. This he did, saying she would be collected in a car, required to make a little speech on stage, and receive a bouquet of flowers. Naturally she accepted, and he arranged the day and pick-up time for the following week. He then telephoned a car-hire company and ordered a car in her name, to take her to the appointed cinema, wait and bring her home again.

On the evening concerned, highly elated, as he always was when playing practical jokes on people, Dennis and I sat in a car near the entrance of Joan's flat in Baker Street, and waited to see the fun begin! The limousine arrived punctually. Out she tripped in full première regalia, followed once more by her long-suffering mother, and away they went.

We were convulsed with laughter and Dennis, whose exuberance knew no bounds, went a step further, and phoned the real manager to warn him that a stage-struck young girl was coming to his cinema, trying to get publicity, and had been causing a great deal of bother with this behaviour for some time.

'Don't worry,' said the manager, as if he had been let in on a spy plot organised by MI5. 'I'll soon deal with her when she gets here.' That was that. We could not be there to see what actually happened as Joan alighted from her car, hand outstretched and smiling, but our guess was that the manager told her in no uncertain terms what to do.

The next morning my telephone rang early, and when I answered I heard a very irate Joan on the other end. It appeared that she had found out who was responsible for the prank, and she was hopping mad, quite naturally. 'If you don't pay for every penny that car cost, I will take you to court,' she screamed.

'Please send me the bill and be my guest,' I said. 'The laugh was well worth the price of a car bill.'

C is for JOAN CRAWFORD

She was an incredible character, strange and puzzling, but whatever else a 'superstar' in her profession!

As stated earlier, we worked together once in a film, and I can only speak from experience, for beneath the dignified, strong exterior was a frightened, lonely woman.

The stories criculating now about Joan Crawford, with the advent of the book written by her adopted daughter entitled *Mommie Dearest*, do tarnish the image a great deal and I find it hard to believe that the same woman who was concerned enough about me to telephone from

Joan and I in 'Berserk'. (1966)

America, when I nearly died of meningitis, is the same one who was capable of being such a monster to her children.

All these terrible tales are possible however if she really was an alcoholic as we are led to believe, and from the various situations I witnessed on the set of the film we made, I am inclined to feel they are true. Despite these there was humour to be found on some occasions. Producer Herman Cohen received an urgent call to her dressing room one day. 'Tell Miss Crawford I am just in the middle of a production meeting,' he said to his secretary, but back came the message that he had better do as he was commanded if he wanted the film to continue. Alarmed as to what the problem might be, Herman hurried to her room and found a thunderous Joan. 'Whatever is wrong?' he asked anxiously, and the whole story unfolded.

As a director of the enormous Pepsi Cola firm, a role she had taken on after the death of her fourth husband Alfred Steel who had originally held the position, Joan decided that everyone on the film should drink as much of the stuff as possible, so she had graciously installed Pepsi Cola machines all over the studio. 'This gesture has been abused,' she announced to a trembling Herman that day. 'But I don't see what the problem is, Joannie,' he cooed in his most sympathetic voice. 'The problem is,' screamed La Crawford, 'that out of the goodness of my heart I have arranged for everyone on this movie to drink Pepsi Cola free and they are treating me with scorn!' 'But Joannie dear,' Herman replied, pretending that even *he* drank the fizzy concoction himself, 'they all love you for it, and they are so grateful, so what is wrong?' 'I'll tell you what's wrong,' she snapped. 'No one is doing me the courtesy of bringing back their empty bottles.'

I do not know exactly how Herman soothed her feathers for she was obsessed by thrifty behaviour, such as saving flower vases which had contained blossoms sent to her, washing them out personally, and flying them back to New York in her luggage. The question then of others saving their 'empties', and returning them, was obviously a major issue in her mind, and I suspect Herman must have promised on oath that instructions would be sent out to everyone that the bottles must be returned on pain of death! After this confrontation not one empty Pepsi Cola bottle was ever seen lying around the set again.

Actor Vincent Price once told me of another obsession she had about writing 'thank you' letters. 'The trouble with Joan is,' he moaned, 'if you send her a Christmas card, she will always write back thanking you for the damned thing, and then expect you to write in answer to *her* letter. When you've done that of course she then writes back again thanking you for your letter to her, and so it goes on.'

Joan Crawford, Oscar winner and actress extraordinaire, had many husbands, lovers, and leading men in her time. What they really felt for her was a matter of conjecture, but certainly they were all undoubtedly in awe of her. British screen actor Michael Wilding left this country with much fear and trepidation, when he went to Hollywood for his first film there starring opposite the great lady.

Being an extremely easy going character, and completely

devoid of temperament, regardless of having married Elizabeth Taylor just before his departure. Michael hoped he would manage to get along fairly well with the tempestuous star. He managed for two days! On the third day, he politely enquired if she was in the habit of attending her previous days' 'rushes' (this is a small collection of the filming done, shown for the actors' benefit if they so desire), whilst they were waiting for the cameras to line up a new scene. 'Yes, but I only go *once*,' replied Joan imperiously, her big eyes narrowing darkly. 'Oh really, why is that?' stammered Michael innocently. 'Not to see myself, for I am always good,' she said, 'but to find out who else might be good, and make sure they never are again!'

D is for BETTE DAVIS

This lady is, to my mind, the greatest actress and screen personality in the world. I have never had the good fortune of meeting her, although we have spoken on the telephone a couple of times in Hollywood when she was trying to negotiate a film contract for my second husband, Richard Dawson. It has always been my ambition to work with her, but up to the time of writing this wish still remains unfulfilled. Like her counterpart Joan Crawford, with whom she appeared in the film *Whatever happened to Baby Jane?*, Bette is one of the last of the giants in Hollywood, they do not make them like her any more.

The personal life of Bette Davis has also been as dramatic as any role she ever played on the screen, but with four marriages behind her it would seem she has decided not to plunge into matrimony again. The last husband, actor Gary Merrill, looked as though he was the right man for a while, but as things turned out he too went the way of the others, and judging from the publicity prior to their divorce, it appears to have been a turbulent union which ended in much bitterness. Bette was heard to say loudly to the press, and anyone else who cared to listen,

'The state of Maine is not big enough for both of us any more,' and presumably on that unhappy note Gary promptly moved away!

This saying, along with her line from the fabulous film *All about Eve* on which she also met and married Gary Merrill, 'Fasten your seat belts, it's going to be a bumpy night,' became almost synonymous with Bette Davis, off screen and on. Never one for being afraid to speak her mind, and as famous for her temperamental outbursts as rival Joan Crawford, it was no wonder that the studio heads trembled in their boots when she signed a contract to make her first film over here in England, with the added clause that newly-wed husband Gary Merrill be given a role in the movie too.

Another Man's Poison was a fairly modest budget production, scheduled to be made at the tiny and rather antiquated studios at Walton-on-Thames, now sadly closed.

Bette was not to know this however when she happily signed to star in the film with her bridegroom, and who could blame her? Walton was a far cry from Warner Brothers.

The honeymooners arrived in a blaze of glory, and actor Anthony Steel, himself then a big star in England, was introduced to the pair as their co-star, but before the film had even really got off the ground trouble started.

Despite her ecstatic marital state Bette was in no mood to put up with amateur behaviour from either technicians or fellow actors, which is what she apparently felt was happening all around her. This was understandable really for although the British cast and crew were doing their best, it was not anywhere near as good as Bette had been used to. To be fair, she had always been a completely efficient professional, whatever anyone else said against her. Somehow she bore the whole ordeal, probably realising that there was nothing she could do about it anyway, but tempers and conditions on the set were tense, and sparks flew on many occasions.

The final day of shooting arrived much to everyone's relief. Bette went through her last scene like the trouper she is, tight-lipped though and obviously unhappy.

The cameras stopped and the director shouted, 'Cut,' rushing over to his star and congratulating her on her performance, whether he meant on screen or off, no one ever knew. The entire crew sat in silence, and Bette asked for a cigarette for which someone hastily proffered a light. 'Well that's it Miss Davis,' said a very nervous studio official. 'The movie is finished, how do you feel?' It was a hideous mistake on his part, especially amidst a silent set, to ask such a question when the actress had been thoroughly miserable about the entire affair, and everyone waited her reply with fervent anticipation.

Looking rather like the heroine from one of her films, Bette eyed him coldly and taking a deep puff of her cigarette, exclaimed in true Davis style, 'Thank God! Now let's get the *hell* out of here!' And so saying she snapped her fingers at the ever attentive Gary Merrill, ground her cigarette into the floor and strode off the set without a backward glance.

D is for DETECTIVE

To most boys, the idea of being a detective has always seemed a much more exciting and adventurous occupation than just being a mere policeman. This is probably due to tales children read about Sherlock Holmes, and of course the heroes they see in films and television who are always on the right side of the law against the bad men.

A 'private' detective has an even more interesting sound but, unlike the slick screen portrayal of Philip Marlowe by the late Dick Powell with its brilliantly crisp dialogue, a private eye in real life is not quite as colourful as he appears.

Many boring hours and sometimes days and nights are spent waiting in wet streets or draughty doorways, often to no avail, for a paltry fee which is a far cry from glossy Hollywood characterisations with big limousines and luxury apartments, such as Richard Roundtree has at his disposal in *Shaft*.

There is also the matter of pleasing the client who is paying for the service, and if the job is not carried through satisfactorily then perhaps the bill does not get paid at all, for customers only want to find out the sort of things with which they can honestly cope.

Jack Hylton, the late theatrical impresario, and Casanova where the ladies were concerned, was just such a client. Back in the Fifties when he had reached the twilight of his life, with silver hair and glasses but still romping around as though he were twenty-one, Jack was well known for generosity towards his mistresses, rather like a modern Charles II. One of these, a swinging redhead named Pat Marlowe, was enjoying all the wealth and easy living his money could buy. He had accommodated her in a beautiful house immediately alongside the Dorchester Hotel, which had once been the exclusive Screenwriters Club, and Jack's only demands on her were two visits a week, which meant she had the rest of the time to amuse herself.

This she did, to the fullest advantage, and as in all the best love triangles Jack was the last to know, but eventually news of Pat's philanderings reached his ears and, fuming with jealousy, he telephoned and instructed a private detective to keep constant watch on the house for one whole week. The man was to report exactly who went in there and what time they came out, for, Jack explained, he was convinced his mistress was deceiving him, and at the price she was costing, he wanted to be sure before giving her the heave ho!

The detective prepared himself for a cold and boring week's work, as it was the middle of winter and even the shelter of the Dorchester Hotel's side entrance was not going to be too comfortable. However, work was work, and unlike all those 'private eyes' he too had seen on the screen waiting in the warm climate of California with comfortable convertible cars, this was to be his assignment, so he had to grin and bear it.

The week passed, and at the end he duly telephoned his

client as arranged. 'Well,' demanded Hylton, 'what have you found out?' 'It's all been very quiet,' he replied. 'You mean to tell me no man has been anywhere near the place,' snapped Hylton suspiciously. 'No sir, no one at all, that you need be worried about,' said the detective triumphantly. 'Only a funny little silver-haired old man with glasses who called twice!'

D is for DIVORCE

Having listened to a television producer friend of mine bemoaning the fact that marriage restricted his sexual activities, and was generally a bore all round, I ventured to ask him exactly why he had ever bothered to get married in the first place. 'It was the great shirt crisis' he answered,

With Bonar Colleano in 'Is Your Honeymoon Really Necessary?'. (1953)

after a few moments' serious deliberation.

I eventually discovered that he, like many other men, had virtually taken a wife, for the simple reason he could not cope with his laundry problems any longer!

Some men marry because they want a good cook, and some just to replace their mothers.

Whatever the logic of it is, marriage seems to be a good idea in the respect that it guarantees them a cook cum housekeeper. Perhaps this is why so many end in divorce?

It is very sad when a marriage which starts off with such hope, crashes in pieces, and I could write at great length on the subject. For the moment however I will keep my observations to myself, and merely quote the words of a very witty friend of mine, who when faced with the prospect of writing a book on the state of matrimony, decided after bitter experience to entitle it, *Marriage is the First Step towards Divorce.*

D is for DOGS

I am not a great dog lover. England is a country full of dog lovers however, to such a degree the general statistics show that people think much more of canine pets, and treat them with a greater amount of kindness than they do their children, a fact which I find disturbing.

I have owned several dogs in my life and they have been adorable, but although it is said that 'dog is man's best friend' I am the kind of person who does not need one leaping all over me each time I walk through the door, covering me with hair and making conversation impossible for five minutes, which is usually the time it takes for them to calm down. Many people love this 'welcome' but personally I prefer the cat, who waits a dignified time to forgive you for going out of the door in the first place, and finally deigns to bestow its favours upon you.

There have been one or two dogs who stand out in my mind as exceptional and I liked them very much. One lovely black labrador named West who lives in the

Donald Sinden and I in 'An Alligator Named Daisy'.

Yorkshire Dales has a small place in my heart, and I also know a pointer in Oxfordshire who is a beautiful fellow.

My husband Alan had a magnificent boxer puppy given to him for his twenty-first birthday, when he was working in a repertory company. Not really the ideal gift for a young actor who earned less than it cost to feed such a champion, and so, reluctantly he was obliged to give it to his mother for safe keeping whilst he continued pursuing his career.

I first met Butch, for that was his name, when I was introduced to Alan's parents before we were married. He had by then grown into the largest boxer I have ever seen, indeed looking more like a bull mastiff with his enormous chest span, but like all fierce-faced dogs, he was an old softie at heart until it came to guarding what was his own.

Upon rising the morning after my introduction to him, I heard a loud barking emanating from beneath the bedroom window and peered out to see what was going on. There in the garden stood Butch, feet planted in an attack position, and chest thrust out indignantly in the direction of the next door cat with whom he waged a ceaseless battle. But it was not the cat he vented his rage on that day, instead, all I could see was a piece of toast on the ground and a few harmless little birds perched in the trees. Listening to his frantic barking and seeing the ferocious look on his face, I called out to my future mother-in-law, 'Whatever is the matter with Butch?' She replied, 'He is a real "dog in the manger"! I threw that piece of toast out for the birds, and although *he* doesn't want it he is *determined* the birds will not have it either!'

Film star Zsa Zsa Gabor works tirelessly and endlessly in Hollywood for the benefit of dogs, a situation I find maudlin, for she could be devoting her time to the care of sick children instead. Katie Boyle, whom I love dearly, carries a Yorkshire terrier, whom I do not love dearly, around in a little basket wherever she goes. I suppose people will always go on fawning over dogs, and no doubt I will upset quite a few dog lovers for daring to write against them at all.

A very amusing story regarding the way a human being can behave stupidly about his canine pet happened at a London theatre in a revue starring the late comedian Sid Field. Each night during the show, which had been running for many months, Sid noticed one of the actors entering a telephone box situated near the stage door and making a brief call. The two things that he thought strange about this were the fact that it always occurred at exactly the same time every evening, and the man never spoke a word whilst inside the phone booth. Unable to restrain his curiosity any longer Sid asked him outright one day who it was that he called each night, and received the answer that the actor's dog was left alone in the flat. So that the dog would not feel unwanted or lonely he would call at a regular time, let his home telephone number ring for a short while, and the dog being extremely intelligent, would then leap about in excitement, for of course it realised that it was his owner calling him from the theatre.

Having had this piece of absurdity explained to him, Sid, who was a great practical joker, decided to pull a fast one on the obviously besotted dog lover.

One evening a few days later, he plotted with a mutual friend to get the actor's front door key and, having done so, arranged that at the time of the telephone call the friend would be at the flat.

Precisely at his usual hour, the actor went as always to the phone and dialled. Sid Field observing him from a hidden vantage point, fell about with laughter at the expression on his face, when having heard the number ring a few times, happily imagining his dog jumping for joy in the normal way, the receiver was suddenly lifted and a gruff voice growled, 'Woof, woof!'

D is for DORIS DAY

A very special lady, and good friend of mine when I first went to Hollywood. We were introduced at a restaurant one evening, and hit it off right away, Doris was then married to her third husband Marty Melcher who died some years ago. Sadly it seems in spite of all his business prowess, he left her, as in the case of Dennis and myself, with many financial debts involving the Taxman.

Whether we got along because we were both blonde, or because our names were almost identical (to such a degree that people often call me Doris instead of Dors in their nervousness), I do not know, but that is really where the comparison finished. Doris is a highly nervous, shy, and insecure person, whilst I, as everyone knows, am the opposite!

'Look at the face,' said the producer who introduced us on the evening concerned. He was speaking of Doris naturally. 'Now that's a face that won't quit.' He was quite right, she has an adorable, tomboy face, alive and twinkling with mischief. Little did I know then that she was hiding an awful lot of sorrow and past distress under her outwardly happy exterior. Doris's autobiography which was published recently told of her terrible first two marriages, rejection by her only son (something she did hint to me that night at dinner), and all the other traumas that have hit her over the years. She has now turned to Christian Science for help and spiritual guidance, amidst the usual scoffing such as I endured when I became a Catholic convert. Indeed I am still experiencing it, for only a little while ago a critic who wanted to make a fast name for himself in journalism wrote in the stately *Sunday Times*, that I had slumped at the foot of the Cross, corpulent and middle-aged.

At the time I met her, Doris had just gone through a major operation for cancer, but despite this was bubbling and cheerful, the way I always imagined her to be. She invited Dennis and me to her home for a dinner party, and when we arrived things really lived up to the publicity I had read. She was, they said, a staunch teetotaller, due no doubt to one alcoholic husband, and there was not a drink in sight. A candy-striped soda fountain stood in one corner of the room where a guest could have whatever took his fancy — soda pop, soft drinks, ice-cream, etc. At dinner, which was elegantly served, there was not a drop of wine to help digest the food, or titillate the palate.

Afterwards we all talked and listened to music, when suddenly something happened which finally made me realise that our likenesses were worlds apart. I had already commented on her wonderful performance in the film *Love Me or Leave Me* with James Cagney, where she played the tragic singing star of the Twenties, Ruth Etting. Doris expressed delight, but explained she had not seen the movie herself! I was somewhat taken aback at this, as I could not imagine anyone being able to stop themselves from at least creeping into the darkened stalls of some suburban cinema to have a look at their performance, no matter how shy they were. 'I have never seen myself on the screen,' she said. 'I went once, to the very first movie I ever made, and that was enough.' I reeled off countless films in which I had seen her, but to each one she shook her head and answered the same way.

At this point her husband Marty came into the room and announced he was going to play her latest record, something she had only just completed. 'Oh God, no!' she cried, and literally fled from the company. It appeared she never listened to herself either, and became a total wreck if someone put on one of her records. This was not an act, it was genuine, and it made me realise that Doris and I were most certainly not the same breed, for if there is one thing I have never been, that is nervous or lacking in confidence. Disgusting, isn't it?

E is for EGOTISM

Generally most people seem to be guilty of this, although in many cases it is quite unconscious, as when signing Christmas cards using only Christian names. The hours, even days, one's brain turns somersaults trying to find out who 'John' is, or why one has received a card from 'Mary', could all have been avoided if only the surname had also been printed, but with complete egotism it seems 'John' or 'Mary' never consider the fact that they are not the only people in the world with these ordinary names!

Harping back to my old theme of knocking the male sex, it has always seemed to me the height of egotism (vanity or conceit, call it what you will), when a man sports a moustache. Some even go to the lengths of wearing their whiskers as long as possible and twirled at the ends! I have often wondered what men would think of women if they were to do the same. How ridiculous we all would look!

By the same token men who wear toupees must take the prize for egotism. If only they would realise that to be bald is much better than being seen balancing a piece of false hair on the top of their heads, usually held in position by some sort of adhesive which is often visible. News-reader Reginald Bosanquet has suffered a great deal of ribbing over his toupee ever since one dreadful day, whilst making a personal appearance at some garden fete, a gust of wind carried it high into the air. Luckily, a courteous gentleman speared it in mid-air with his shooting stick, thus saving the wretched object, but not I should imagine, Reggie's blushes!

In the good old days before my ego was deflated.

If I thought that the whole country knew I was appearing on television with something false like Reggie, in my case, say a pair of 'padded boobs', then there would be no way I could possibly continue the masquerade. But then I am speaking for myself and cannot answer for the behaviour of men and their vanities.

A classic example of egotism happened once when I was making a film which was being directed by an old friend who was originally a Cockney con man when I met him first in South Africa in 1958. However, since that time he had come up in the world, and having the gift of the gab, talked himself into films and subsequently directing. By the time we met again he had made several celluloid romps which he did not hesitate to boast about, although his claim to being one of the five top British film directors, along with Sir Carol Reed and David Lean, fell far short of the truth.

We were on location at Billingsgate Fish Market, not an altogether glamorous spot, but necessary for the plot of the film which was a comedy. Having settled into my dressing room trailer on the opening day of shooting I watched him with some amusement, rushing around, shouting orders to the camera crew and generally behaving in the way he considered a top film director should. Eventually he entered my trailer and throwing himself into an armchair, excitedly began telling me for the hundredth time of his great prowess as a film tycoon, and how fortunate I was to be given the opportunity to work with him on his new venture.

'It is amazing how far you have come since the old days', I humoured him by saying, but he interrupted without giving me a chance to finish. 'Yes, yes. Do you know I came down here yesterday to inspect the location and started talking to the fish porters', he announced. 'It suddenly made me aware of something about myself which I had not come to terms with.' 'And what was that?' I enquired guardedly. 'Over these last successful years I have completely lost touch with the *working* classes,' he replied pompously.

To be fair, not only men are guilty of egotism. A

daughter of one of our leading theatrical impresarios, now long since passed on, was berating a small part actor in the show that her father was presenting in London. She had been cast to appear in it herself, in his attempt to launch her as an actress. The impresario stood hidden in the wings for a while as his spoilt young daughter ticked the poor actor off for a minor mistake he had made, informing him that as she was 'who' she was, he had better watch out in the future! When she finished her tirade and stalked off, her father walked up to the crestfallen fellow and said consolingly, 'Please take no notice of my daughter. I am afraid she is far too full of *my* importance!'

The boot can be on the other foot where children are concerned though, for if any parent nourishes the slightest hint of too much ego, then children are surely the ones who will cut them down to size. Happily I do not have an enormous ego, and therefore can safely say I am not guilty of displaying much egotism, but I suppose there are occasions when I do get carried away with myself if

Jason doing it at the fête.

flattered enough. This happened when I was invited a few years ago to attend a garden fete. As is often the case with personal appearances of this kind by celebrities, I had been offered a small fee for doing so, and accepted happily, informing them that I would also bring my husband and five-year-old son Jason along, as there was a children's fancy dress competition which I thought they could help me judge. All in all I felt it would help to make a charming domestic picture!

Things went very well and Jason did his bit, prettily presenting the children with their prizes and helping to hand out other cups and medals for adults besides. There was a great fuss made of me as always on these occasions, photographs taken and compliments flying everywhere, all of which perhaps went to my head a little. Puffed up with my own importance, it came as a shock, whilst wallowing in supreme egotism, when Jason who was becoming rather bored with the proceedings tugged at my arm just as I was in the middle of a rather magnanimous speech regarding the aspects of personal appearances, and boomed through the microphone for everyone to hear, 'Mummy . . . How much are you getting paid for doing this?'

No sooner had I recovered from this embarrassing situation, when I received the final thrust guaranteed to deflate any ego which I may have had left that afternoon. A woman rushed out of the crowd waving a piece of paper for me to autograph, saying, 'I knew it must be *you* Diana . . . because I recognised your husband!'

E is for EQUITY

To those not in show business this word has a totally different meaning, but for we actors it represents a union which operates solely for the benefit of looking after our interests, namely keeping us safe from phoney managements, theatrical companies whose financial backing does not live up to their verbal protestations, and film producers who try to extract every last ounce of energy and talent from us without paying all they should for the service.

Some artistes like myself would actually prefer *not* to be forced to join however. If I have any trouble with bogus companies, I would rather fight my own battles, but unfortunately even actors have to have a union in Britain today, it is compulsory, and if they want to be in show business, they must pay their annual dues to Equity or never be allowed to work.

I am not the only person who resents being made to belong to something against my will. Indeed I remember actor David Tomlinson some twenty years ago when appearing with me in a film entitled *Is Your Honeymoon Really Necessary?*, bitterly opposing the fact that he had to pay his dues to Equity and practically causing a 'sit down strike' on the set as a result, before he was finally carried kicking and struggling to his cheque book.

In its own way I suppose the idea is good in principle, and for certain actors who cannot afford to fight for themselves it is marvellous, but there are of course people like Vanessa Redgrave and brother Corin, amongst others, who try to persuade all actors to join the left wing Workers' Revolutionary Party and take things to an extreme. This naturally sullies the whole theory, turning everything in the direction of Communism, and consequently hindering matters instead of helping them.

Regardless of Miss Redgrave and her Red Square ambitions, as stated, every artiste involved in any branch of show business must pay up and join, which brings me to Equity's latest recruit, none other than that well-known boyfriend of 'you know who', Roddy Llewellyn, who has also had to become part of the hallowed membership . . . the reason given for this, somebody quipped, is because he has a small part in *Charley's Aunt!*

My horses exercising me.

E is for EXERCISE

Ugh! and I do mean ugh! Some people enjoy it and good
luck to them. Indeed I once had a muscle-bound boyfriend
whose main occupation was lifting weights and generally

Arm wrestling with Primo Carnera in 'A Kid for Two Farthings'. (1954)

exercising his biceps. This undoubtedly made *him* happy, but it was very boring for me, as it was impossible to conduct a conversation with all that deep breathing and panting going on, and frankly it also tired him out for other more interesting pastimes!

From childhood I have always hated the idea of exercise,

on the netball field at school I would be seen sauntering along, hands dug into the pockets of my shorts, not giving a hoot whether the wretched ball went in the net or not.

Gymnasiums positively appalled me. Furthermore I considered them highly dangerous and used to inveigle my mother into writing notes using various excuses as to why I could not take part in the weekly classes.

Games have never appealed to me much, physical ones that is! Except perhaps a casual set of tennis.

And as for walking? . . . Heaven forbid I should ever have to vacate my car and 'hoof' it any time, which does remind me of the Jewish joke about two mothers discussing their sons' methods of getting to school. One said that her son walked there every day, and asked why the other child always arrived in a Rolls Bentley, 'Can't he walk?' she said. 'Thank God he doesn't have to!' exclaimed his mother!

E is for EXPERIENCE

This is a very important thing for any young aspiring actor or actress to acquire. If one is starting out on a career in the theatre, the first question asked by an agent, producer or casting director is, 'What experience have you had?' and if the answer is, 'None,' the young hopeful will be told to go away, acquire some, and stop wasting everybody's time!

When I left the London Academy of Music and Dramatic Art where I was trained, to begin the long trek around agents' offices, I was quite prepared for all this and felt suitably ready to cope, as I was proudly armed with my gold medal and diploma for acting. Imagine my surprise when asked by the head of contract artistes at the J. Arthur Rank organisation what experience I'd had, and having informed him of my hard earned attainments, I was met with a blank stare, and the reply,' Oh really. What else have you done?'

Probably the best story regarding experience concerns that craziest of all millionaire pop stars, the late Keith

Moon, known to everyone as 'Moon the Loon', due to his wild and eccentric behaviour.

During his brief life span, Mooney was ejected many times from noble establishments throughout the world, but happily when he decided to smash up an exclusive hotel suite, or wreck a party reception, he had plenty of money to pay for the damage he had done.

Owner of many beautiful cars, he also had a penchant for driving the vehicles into swimming pools and leaving them to rust. No one really knew why he felt the desire to do this, so it was no surprise when composer Lionel Bart told me that one day whilst driving down Sunset Boulevard in a Rolls Royce with Mooney, he heard him order his chauffeur to drive into the elegant Beverly Hilton Hotel, straight up the steps, through the lobby, and park in the pool beyond.

Lionel was not over-excited about the idea of meeting his end in a watery grave like this, and hoped the chauffeur would ignore Mooney's command, but to his horror the man did exactly as he was bid, and they ploughed through the hotel lobby, scattering people right and left!

As the ornate glass doors leading to the swimming pool were smashed asunder, Lionel figured the moment had come for a quick escape, so wrenching open the car door he tried in vain to get out, but all to no avail. Down he went in style, and to use his own words, 'That was it, Di darling. Glug. Glug. Glug.'

What happened next was quite remarkable, for as he dragged himself out soaking wet, there, standing at the side of the pool was Mooney, bone dry, champagne glass in hand, with not a drop spilt! 'However did you manage to get out?' gasped Lionel, unable to believe the entire sequence of events, for the chauffeur was now floating in a sea of bubbles.

'Experience dear boy,' replied Mooney loftily, 'experience.'

F is for BRUCE FORSYTH

Of all the talented personalities England has ever produced I rate Bruce Forsyth as one of the greatest, and obviously from the success of his television shows, a few million other people think the same. It is strange that in this country we never seem to have had the 'giant' comedians such as America has, in the style of Jack Benny, Bob Hope, Groucho Marx, etc. etc. There have been and still are in England many comedians who all provide laughter and enjoyment in their own way, but to my mind only a handful can be placed among the 'greats,' and Bruce is certainly one of them.

I have known him for a long time now, and on the occasions we have worked together, his talent for doing *anything* extremely well never ceased to amaze me.

Socially, Bruce before his marriage to Anthea, and after the break-up with his first wife, was a regular guest at my home for parties or small gatherings. Many a good laugh was had in those days, but none funnier than the night we lined up a 'blind date' for Bruce, who was usually without a girlfriend anyway, female company seeming to take second place to his true love, golf!

The night Bruce's blind date was arranged happened in Stockton where he was appearing in cabaret. I too was doing my nightclub act in the same vicinity, and the comedy team of Kenny Earle and Malcolm Vaughn were likewise knocking audiences sideways at yet another place named The Top Hat Club, which with all due respect was not quite in the same league as the venues where Bruce and I were appearing. I say this, because on the bill with Kenny and Malcolm was a 'drag' act who had styled himself on *me*, and whilst he gave the Top Hat audiences what they wanted, was not the type of performer who would make Danny La Rue nervous!

We were all staying at the same hotel, which was pleasant, as it meant that during the long and rather lonely days, we could get together for lunch and good conversation. The same applied at night, for when we all returned from our various engagements, with the

With Tommy Cooper, another one of the greats — just like that!

adrenalin still flowing, we would gather in my suite until dawn.

Kenny Earle was concerned about Bruce's love life! He never seemed to have a date, but there was nothing any of us could do about it, for there was no eligible female around. Never one for missing a trick, Kenny hit on the idea of lining him up with the 'drag' act from his club, and told Bruce when we had all come back to my suite that night, that there would be a fabulous blonde awaiting his pleasure, and he was sure Bruce would be mad about 'her'.

Knowing who the 'girl' was we looked forward with immense delight to the scene which lay ahead, and Bruce although trying to appear nonchalant, was obviously looking foward to it too.

Around 1.30 a.m. we all assembled in the hotel. Drinks and food were organised, and we noticed that Bruce had dressed in something smarter than his usual 'back from the club' type clothes.

The time went by but no date arrived, and at about 2.15

with Kenny fidgeting conspicuously and assuring us that Bruce's date would definitely be coming, I suggested we passed the endless waiting by having a seance. This to anyone who is an amateur in the occult world, as we all were, involves placing the letters of the alphabet around a polished table, and using an upturned wine glass on which everyone places a finger, asking questions, and hoping the glass, via the spirits, will spell out the answers.

The idea was greeted with enthusiasm, though Bruce was clearly very disappointed that his evening was going to wind up in a totally different way from that which he had envisaged. Instead of a dream girl, he was going to get a dream world!

After the initial start, and a few silly questions being asked, whilst the glass slid about all over the table, Kenny with the air of a mischievous pixie enquired in a demanding voice, 'Will Bruce Forsyth's date arrive tonight?' At this precise moment the door burst open, frightening us all out of our wits as it was so unexpected, and there stood Bruce's date in all her glory, false eyelashes, black negligee, and purring sexily, 'I'm here darlings.'

Apart from the incredible timing of her arrival which in no way could have been planned as it had happened, we were amazed at the impact and appearance, and Bruce was breathless, unable to believe that Kenny had found such a raving beauty there in the wilds of the countryside.

An appalling hour followed however, as he tried to make some sort of contact, but at every twist and turn the naughty deceiver managed to keep him in a state of utter frustration, until finally worn out and defeated by 4 a.m. Bruce gave up the whole thing, and went sadly to his bed.

Kenny could still not resist letting the night end without one further prank though, and after paying the 'lady' a couple of pounds for the amusement she had given by playing her part so well, told her to pop along to Bruce's room, knock on the door, and just say 'goodnight.' Off she went adjusting her falsies, and Kenny played his last hand. 'Dorsey,' he cried, 'Get on the phone to the hall porter and complain that Bruce Forsyth has got a prostitute in his bedroom.' Needing no second bidding I did just that, stating indignantly that I thought it was a *respectable* hotel, and why were people like Bruce Forsyth allowed to behave in such a disgraceful manner simply because they were stars? The porter came running up the stairs at the precise moment when Bruce was saying goodnight to his somewhat bizarre date, and the scene to the porter's eyes was exactly that which I had complained about so bitterly, particularly as the lady in question was wearing transparent black underwear.

A rather heated fracas followed, not helped by the fact that the drag queen did not like being ejected in this way, so delighted was he with his performance, that to be man-handled down the corridor by a mere hall porter was not his idea of a good finale! Malcolm Vaughn who had dashed to his own room, stood by the door shouting in outraged Welsh tones, 'Disgusting, who does that Forsyth think he is bringing women like that into the hotel at this time of night?' Bruce tried vainly to shush him, but then the worst happened! In the melée, the drag queen's rubber boobs came off in the porter's hands, and hysterically tearing off his wig he shrieked, 'I'm not a bloody woman anyway. I'm a man!'

I do not know who looked more astounded and embarrassed, the porter or Bruce, who bolted back into his room and was not seen by anyone for several days . . . I think he forgave us eventually, but for the rest of that memorable week he steered clear of the night porter, and any more offers to line him up with a blind date.

F is for FAUX PAS

A French expression meaning an embarrassing mistake, error or blunder. All of us have been guilty of this at some time or other. I have had to think quickly or talk myself out of a hot situation often, but by the same token there have been instances when someone has either meaningfully or unconsciously made a faux pas or two with me.

Watching Sammy Davies at work.

During the publicity promotion tour for my last book, I met literally hundreds of people — book salesmen, their wives, directors of wholesale bookshops, printers, and naturally the buying public themselves. I have found over the years that people when nervous do tend to say the most incredible things, and as a large number were in this state when they met me at the signing sessions and cocktail parties, a couple of very embarrassing faux pas occurred.

The first was intentional, as is often the case when men confront me, egged on by their friends sniggering in the background. A young man approached with a copy of my

71

book in his hand and a sly grin on his face saying, 'Perhaps you would be kind enough to sign this for my father Miss Dors. He has always been a great fan of yours.'

I took the book and prepared to write by asking his father's name. 'Oh don't bother about that,' he exclaimed. 'Just put . . . in memory of many happy orgasms. That will make his day!' 'Well it certainly will not make mine,' I said angrily, shoving the book back at him without bothering to write my signature.

At the other end of the scale I encountered on the same tour a young man who unlike the previous oaf, was falling over himself to please and be polite. As I signed my autograph, he nervously chattered on about nothing, and in one last effort to flatter me, remarked on my golden sun tan. I thanked him, and he went on to stammer, 'What a beautiful colour, obviously you have just come back from sunny climaxes.' Thankfully he never realised his unfortunate mispronunciation, and I managed to keep my face straight in order to save his!

Another typical faux pas many famous people encounter is that made by fans who twist their sentence around in confusion, and gush glowingly, 'I really think you're wonderful. Yes, *you've* always been a great fan of *mine.*'

This can be excused really, for nine times out of ten the excited person does not even realise they have made a blunder. I knew that *I* had made one however, with Sammy Davis Jnr. on our first meeting when we appeared in the Royal Command Performance of 1960.

Sammy had flown from America that very day and plunged into heavy rehearsals, which exhausted him and it was beginning to show. 'Try and get some sleep,' I advised. 'It's terrible to expect all this from someone. They've been working you like a *black!*'

Probably the worst faux pas I ever heard about, was a deliberate remark to embarrass actress Lilli Palmer, when she was making a personal appearance in connection with her autobiography at a cocktail party.

As Lilli graciously signed her books and talked courteously with everyone, a man loomed up to her and bellowed, 'Tell me Miss Palmer, is it right that you were married to Rex Harrison once?' 'Indeed I was,' said Lilli, a trifle tight-lipped at the mention of her ex-husband, even though it had been a long time before. 'Then perhaps you will tell me if what I hear about about him is true,' went on the offender blatantly. 'Has he really got the biggest one in show business?'

F is for FETISH

I suppose everyone has some sort of fetish, perhaps without even knowing it. My own particular thing is anything 'shiny'. As a child I was fascinated by cellophane paper, which at the time girls were making into waist belts, so it seems I was not alone in my liking for it. I also adored, and still do, patent leather shoes. Having analysed my own fetish, I realise I am amongst the lucky ones whose secret thrill at touching certain items is really quite harmless, and does not lead to sexual problems or hang ups.

If a fetish is to do with merely liking the feel of something, or the necessity of wearing types of clothes, in some cases rubber garments, then it is relatively harmless, but when sexual perversion comes into the matter things take a more serious turn.

I have heard some strange cases in my time, although I hasten to say most of the stories related to me were usually second hand from the experiences of prostitutes. More vivid however, were actual newspaper articles concerning stars like Dan Dailey and George Maharis, who had both been picked up by police in Hollywood on 'different occasions, for walking around in women's clothing. Indeed I even saw a cover picture on the front of *Confidential* magazine once, where the late Duke of Windsor had been photographed in 'drag'.

Oddly enough, at the time all this was being published in Hollywood, I happened to be lunching one day at 'The Luau' restaurant, when I spotted actor Peter Sellers at a

Peter Reynolds and I in 'Manbait'. (1951)

corner table with a beautiful young girl. He smiled and
waved, but it was obvious they were deep in conversation
and did not wish to be disturbed, so I did not go over and
speak to them.

The next day my telephone rang and it was Peter, a little
concerned at not having had a chat the previous day. I
assured him it did not matter as I realised he was on a
'heavy' date, and inquired how he had got along with his new
girlfriend. Peter laughed heartily. 'What a weirdo she turned
out to be,' he said. 'Do you know? All she was
interested in doing when we got back to the hotel suite was
washing my hair!' 'That's a strange fetish,' I replied,
imagining the comical sight of Peter Sellers with his head in
a basin full of soapy water, instead of behaving like the
Casanova he portrayed in a film we did together entitled
There's a Girl in my Soup. 'Well I did my best to talk her
out of it,' he sighed, 'But she did not want to know, and I
think I must have the cleanest hair in Hollywood.'

As far as actually making love is concerned, fetishes and

fantasies seem to go hand in hand at times. One American screen hero's big sexual delight was to be handcuffed to the bed before anything got started. The late John Garfield could only find stimulation with coloured whores before he died so tragically, and England's Stewart Granger once confessed to me at a dinner party where we were seriously discussing sex, that his best fantasy was to be made love to by a large woman who looked rather like his nanny, thus reverting back to childhood I presume.

My dear friend, the late Peter Reynolds, had an extraordinary encounter with fetishism during his early youth in Hampstead. At the time he was flat broke as actors tend to be occasionally, so when asked by a stranger if he would be prepared to attend a party dressed as an S.S. officer for a sum of money, he happily agreed to do so.

Upon arrival at the house he perceived a group of Jewish people all wearing the kind of striped apparel worn by prisoners in camps such as Belsen and Dachau, with large stars on their backs. The man who had made him the offer in the first place then handed him a large whip and told him to beat them all, using every Jewish insult he could think of whilst doing so. Amazed and rather shocked Peter was obliged to do this macabre and sinister task simply because he needed the money. He did not enjoy himself at all, but his 'victims' thoroughly relished their evening and writhed around the floor wallowing in glorious self-debasement!

The closest I ever got to fetishism was on one occasion when I answered a ring at the front door not long after my first book had been highly publicised in a national newspaper serialisation. It was a custom of mine never to actually open the door but peep through the window alongside, and as I did so I saw a man standing in the driveway holding up a very gaudy looking dinner jacket in a plastic bag.

'Miss Dors, forgive me for bothering you,' he began, 'but I wondered if you might be interested in buying this?' Not understanding why he thought I would even remotely consider paying good money for an article of men's clothing I replied, 'Not really. What gave you the idea of coming here with it in the first place?' 'Forgive me,' he fawned, 'but you see it belonged to Tom Jones, when he last appeared at the London Palladium.' Standing back proudly he indicated the monstrosity with its sequin lapels and brightly coloured lining. 'I'm sure it did from the look of it,' I observed dryly, 'but I still fail to see what that has to do with me.' The man looked mischievous, 'Well Miss Dors,' he persisted, 'I've no further use for it, and just recently I read in the newspaper series that you liked him a great deal, so naturally I thought *you* might like to have the feel of it too.'

The answer he received after this last bit of reasoning is not printable here, even under the title of fetish.

G is for GEMINI

The most irritating sign of the zodiac for Scorpios like myself, say the authorities in astro circles, and it is true. Geminis are so influenced by the twins who preside over their sign, that whether they like it or not, they are forced to lead double lives and never know which twin they are going to be from day to day, the good or the bad, consequently making life very difficult for those around them. It is odd really, because even though my sign is not supposed to get along too well with them, I have many close friends who are Geminis, and although I love each one dearly, they aggravate the hell out of me at times!

G is for GHOSTS

Being a Scorpio I am fascinated by subjects concerning the supernatural. Unfortunately, and I use the word with care, I have never actually seen a ghost, yet on one occasion perhaps I did?

It was whilst driving back across the Pennines, an eerie

With Alfred Hitchcock, master of the supernatural, on the set of 'Run for Doom'. (1963)

place to be at night, that my companion and I saw a woman walking towards us on the other side of the road wearing a grey cloak and hood. Under normal circumstances this would not have been unusual, but it was around two in the morning, a cold, wet, black night, and not the sort of weather in which anyone would care to take a stroll! We had been travelling quite a distance before encountering her and there were no signs of other life around at all. As she passed us I thought it strange a woman should be out alone at that time, but upon journeying further I also noted that there were no houses or buildings for many miles.

'How odd,' I said. 'Where could she be going? It is completely remote up here.' 'I have no idea,' replied my companion. 'And what is more, I do not want to know!'

Whether this was my only contact with a ghost I will

never know, but the more I think about the situation, the cloak and hood she wore, which is not the type of clothing seen in this day and age, the more I am convinced that it probably might well have been.

Until this brief incident my interest in the supernatural had not extended far beyond holding amateur seances with a Ouija board, which is, I may add, a very dangerous thing to do!

Whether there is really anything to the Ouija scene I do not know, but I have had some amazing answers in the past, and there seems to be no explanation for it.

Years ago I owned a fifteenth-century farm, so the atmosphere was excellent for games of this kind. One evening a group of friends and myself sat at a table, having a seance and delving into the subject of reincarnation. We asked the spirit who professed to be with us, if we had all lived before in a previous life, and firstly it refused to answer, saying there was no such thing as reincarnation! Disappointed by this, as we were all convinced it was wrong, we persisted in our questioning and eventually received the spelt out reply, 'Not reincarnation. Everlasting life.'

Somewhat taken aback by this, but intrigued to find out who we might have been before, we phrased the questions carefully and found out some odd facts about ourselves. One girl well known to be desperately fond of horses, was reputed to have actually been a horse belonging to a knight in days of old. Another girl had been an Arabian princess in the desert, one man had been a convict who died of scurvy on his way to deportation in Australia, and yet another had, to use the words spelt that night, 'Died in pit. As a warrior.'

Naturally I was anxious to know about my own fate in a previous life, but each time I enquired, the pointer flew to the word 'no' and it was apparent that the thing did not want to tell me. Finally I *demanded* to know as everyone had been answered satisfactorily, and I was somewhat annoyed at its reluctance. Slowly the words spelt out, 'Whore, in Dickens's era, died diseased.'

Well I had asked for it! and I could only assume the

spirit had tried to spare my feelings, but on the next occasion a few weeks later when I introduced the Ouija board game to comedy actor Bill Maynard in a dressing room at the Liverpool Empire where we were both appearing, we got on to the subject of previous existences and yet again it revealed the awful truth about *me*. Happily, Bill came off a little better I might add, his life had been that of an Egyptian retainer to some ancient king and, as was the custom then, had been buried alive within the tomb when his master died.

After all this interest in the supernatural, I went back to work in Hollywood again, and introduced the Ouija board to a number of people over there, among them singer Dorothy Squires, who was then married to Roger Moore. I had known them both for ten years, having first met Dot in Blackpool with my late husband Dennis Hamilton, and he and Roger had also been close friends during his lifetime. Dot was a little dumbfounded at first when she and I sat together trying to contact the spirits, as for fifteen minutes nothing happened at all. 'What is it supposed to do?' she asked. 'Just hold on Dot,' I replied. 'When it eventually gets warmed up and we've contacted someone you will be astounded. Maybe the atmosphere of Hollywood is not as good as my old farm in England.'

After waiting a little longer the pointer began to move, and to our surprise we made contact with none other than Dennis himself. Dot was amazed, and having asked a number of questions which he appeared to answer correctly as to where she had met him and so on, she announced excitedly to Roger, who would have nothing to do with it, 'Here Roger. We've got Dennis Hamilton on this thing.' Roger looked sceptical and scoffed, 'Rubbish! Tell you what, if it really is Hamilton ask him about the pound bet we had together, he'll know what I mean.' 'What bet was that?' demanded Dot. 'Just something that happened once,' he said. 'Go on, ask him,' and he smirked disbelievingly. Dot and I did as he ordered not knowing what he was talking about, and to our utter astonishment a story unfolded about an occasion when Dennis and Roger had climbed in through the window of television producer

Dennis Vance's house at Windsor; the breaking of glass; and a monetary bet of a pound which had been involved for some reason. Roger, who up to that moment had been sneering about the merits of my Ouija board, went deathly white in colour for the story was absolutely true! Since that day I have also checked with Dennis Vance himself, together with his son Patrick who was there at the time, and it is completely correct!

So much for amateur seances. But what about ghosts, ghouls and things that go bump in the night?

I once rented a house near Ascot which was definitely haunted. The previous owners had been friends of mine. One of them, a young pianist, had committed suicide a few years before but he had experienced his happiest times during his lifetime living there. The first person to discover anything uncanny, was actor Andrew Ray, who had been spending Christmas there with a few other friends and myself. Having retired to bed, he suddenly came rushing down the corridor and rapped on my door. 'Diana, please wake up,' he cried. 'I think I've just seen a ghost.' It appeared that he was lying in bed trying to get to sleep, when he perceived a man dressed in grey enter the room and step behind the door as if hiding. Thinking it was one of the men in the house playing tricks, Andrew pleaded, 'Come on now. Stop trying to give me the horrors,' upon which the man stepped forward and brushed something which felt like a balloon in his face. Andrew sat bolt upright and turned on the lamp, but no one was there, the room was empty!

After this we all became aware of strange instances occurring as the weeks went by. The bedroom used by Andrew, and empty most of the time, was tidied up every day by my cleaning woman. Quite innocently she told me that each morning it was necessary to straighten the bedcover, as although no one had used the bed it was always wrinkled and crumpled.

Actress Sandra Dorne was seated at her dressing table in another room one day, when she heard someone knock on the door, and thinking it was the cleaning woman shouted, 'Come in', several times. Finally, obtaining no response, she went to the door only to find the woman was not even there! Sandra's little French poodle also reacted very strongly to the house, and on one occasion actually scratched at the door of the room with its paws, until they bled, in an effort to get at something unseen.

Andrew Ray's daughter, who was then only two or three, later spoke in childish awe of 'the nice man in grey' she had seen several times in her bedroom, and one night my two dogs who had been locked up as usual in the kitchen, were found next morning in the drawing room, when they had no way of gaining access to it.

If these odd happenings were the work of a ghost then it was obviously only a mischievous one, and the final prank played on us was when a bread knife went missing one day, which caused great inconvenience as we had to try to slice a loaf with an ordinary knife. We did not discover the original until the next day, sticking straight up out of a flower pot at the end of the garden! If this had been a joke played by one of my guests then it was certainly a very feeble effort.

The house I live in now is built on what was originally hallowed ground, and we keep finding relics of beautiful stones with religious paintings on them in the garden near a monks' walk. Originally there was a monastery here which presumably suffered at the hands of either Henry VIII or Cromwell, and we have all experienced strange sounds like the trudge of sandalled feet upstairs, celestial singing late at night, and many other curious incidents, all of which add up to the place being haunted, possibly by one of the monks who lived here. Indeed, a friend of mine who was certainly not a believer in ghosts, saw the long robes and sandals of a man disappearing around the corner of his room one night when he stayed there.

This piece brings us inevitably to spiritualists, clairvoyants and fortune-tellers. I have known several good ones over the years; the late Maurice Woodruff, and another named Dalinda, living now in Scotland, who read my hand and told of my past and future more accurately than anyone has ever done. Years ago I was introduced to an amazing Jewish spiritualist named Joseph Benjamin

With Des O'Connor and Lonnie Donegan.

who still conducts meetings twice a week in London. For a small fee he would come to my house and put on a marvellous display of spiritualism, bringing back people's dead relatives, spying any number of ghosts wandering about the living room, and generally giving everyone news and information, hot from the 'other side'!

One evening amongst those invited to witness Joe's incredible powers, was comedian Jon Pertwee, who had brought along a young dancer named Gillian Vaughn as his date. Joe went into his usual trance, informing us through the spirits of what we had done and what we were about to do, but Jon was very sceptical regarding the whole matter. Each time Joe made a reference to his past he succeeded in disproving him, something which did not go down too well with the spiritualist.

The evening wore on and admittedly Joe did provide some quite devastating facts, although come to think of it, he did not tell the aforementioned Gillian that she would eventually marry a comedian, not Jon, but Des O'Connor!

Finally, after one last rather heated argument with Joe over his knowledge of the 'other side', Jon decided it was time to leave, and bade us all a curt 'goodnight', muttering to me as he left that he thought the man was a complete fraud, and not very entertaining either! Whether or not Joe actually overheard Jon's last statement, I do not know, but turning to the remaining guests he announced triumphantly, 'That Pertwee didn't like me, and he had good reason not to. He was afraid I'd reveal him through my powers for what I think he really is . . . A Jew, and a pouff!'

G is for GAMBLING

This is probably the worst sickness of all. I have always maintained that a drug addict need only take a certain amount of drugs, and an alcoholic take one drink too many, before both collapse under the influence of their respective poisons.

A gambler, on the other hand, can and does, go on ad infinitum. There is no limit to his gambling for somehow he will find money from any source with which to bet. The late Lord Byron lost his entire fortune on the turn of a card. Many have been sent to prison for embezzlement due to losing heavily at the races, and I once knew a man who was so addicted to gambling it had completely destroyed his marriage. Finally, in a last attempt to save it, he gave his wife a sum of money with which to pay their living expenses, and ordered her *never* to let him get his hands on it at any time, no matter how much he pleaded or threatened.

The worst ultimately happened of course, as it always does to an inveterate gambler. Down on his luck once again, he begged his wife to forget what he had previously said, because he explained there was a *sure* winner in a horse race, and he could, he promised, get out of trouble completely with the prize money. His poor wife steadfastly refused, thinking she was doing the right thing, but after a terrible argument he became so desperate, that he seized

Helping my husband to lose $60,000.

their baby and threatened meaningfully to throw it on the fire if she did not give him the money.

This of course was definitely the end of the marriage, and he wound up broke and ruined.

I have had the odd bet on races, and enjoyed many a game of cards, particularly poker, but happily I am not a gambler, and like my husband Alan consider money is too hard to come by to be frittered away on reckless gambling; the odds of winning being well against punters most of the time. It is of course very easy to squander someone else's money, as one boyfriend of mine did years ago! And whilst he reigned, money was gambled and lost at race meetings and poker games most of the time.

I would hear tales of so called 'systems' he had invented to win money at gambling clubs and race courses, and even allowed myself, together with some of our friends, to be drawn into these 'get rich quick' schemes, each time only to realise sadly that there is no infallible way of winning. One incredible evening at some dog track, a cat was held in wait by a few villain friends he knew, to be thrown in front of the winning dog, should it be the wrong one nearing the finishing post. Apparently the cat was sent hurtling through the air and caused the entire race to end in complete chaos with greyhounds running in all directions! But still he did not win.

During my association with him some very strange card games were organised at my home, and whilst he battled to win money, I observed with great amusement, the tricks he and a friend would employ.

Perhaps the funniest was on one occasion when he had invited some rich 'chinless wonders' as he called them, along for a game of poker. Before their arrival he had 'fixed' another deck of cards in case the game went against him, and naturally they were arranged in his favour so that he would scoop the pot. The plan was that if the game went down financially for him, as it usually did, he would ask his friend to go and make a snack in the kitchen where the fixed cards had been left. At a given signal the friend was to drop something, making a loud enough noise to ensure everyone would jump. He would then rush out to see what it was and change packs, returning immediately to deal as normal.

The 'chinless wonders' arrived and the game proceeded. As he had pessimistically surmised, things did not go well for either him or his friend, who was wiped out of the game quite early on, losing a wager of some eight hundred pounds! Finally he decided the time had come for the 'bent' game. Asking his friend to go and make a snack, he carefully waited until the moment arrived for him to deal, and as planned, gave the signal by coughing loudly. There emanated from the kitchen the loudest crash I have ever heard, which was caused by his friend dropping every saucepan he could find in there to really make it a good one! 'What's that idiot done now?' cried my boyfriend rushing out, pack in hand. Quickly they changed cards and back he came in a trice, berating his accomplice for being so clumsy. He then dealt the fixed pack and naturally won the pot. All of which goes to show that in the world of gambling, there might always be a cheater at the table.

Stories of attempted ploys by people in Las Vegas, the gambling city of the world, make my boyfriend's amateur tricks with saucepans look pretty silly, but suffice to say it seems everyone is 'at it' if given the chance. However, it was not a trick on my husband Alan's part once when we were staying there, that prompted him to place a large bet on a certain number at the roulette table. Like myself, not being a gambler, he was uneasy at having been lured to the wretched game in the first instance, but when his number came up he was naturally delighted and relieved. Flushed with success at his luck, he toyed with the idea of putting all the winning money on number 'thirty-five' and asked my advice as to whether he should do so. Horrified, I quickly talked him out of it, saying there was no way he could possibly have two winning numbers in such rapid succession. Reluctantly he walked away from the table, but unable to resist finding out what the result would have been, he hung around until the wheel stopped spinning. 'Thirty five,' called the croupier triumphantly as there was no one betting on it, including Alan.

I have never been able to live down that night in Las

Vegas when, although my husband is not a gambler, I caused him to lose about sixty thousand dollars.

G is for BETTY GRABLE

I was appearing in cabaret in Las Vegas in 1960, when I first met Betty. She was doing a show too, but also lived there permanently with her adored husband Harry James, the band leader. We hit it off right away, and every time I went back to Vegas either to work or play, we would always get together and have good times. Betty's idea of a really enjoyable evening however, would be for us to go and sit in the lounge of the Flamingo Hotel where Harry James was playing most of the year, and just listen to him.

La Grable was a star in the true sense of the word, but like all true stars she was the last person to think that way about herself and never pulled the star routine on anyone. One of the things we had in common, was that she felt as I did about the tiring aspect of two shows a night in Las Vegas. She would arrive at the club, with her hair in rollers hidden under a headscarf, and begin the tedious business of getting made-up, when really all she felt like doing was staying home and watching television. She used to say, 'Diana, I never feel I can get through the evening, but as soon as the damn shows are over I come alive, and I'm ready to go to the first party anyone suggests.'

I knew exactly what she meant, as it is a recognised fact that once the adrenalin begins moving on stage, any performer brightens up no matter how bad they feel at the start.

One evening a rather nasty incident happened to Betty and me. Neither of us were working at the time, so we decided to go out on the town with two male dancers we knew, because in Las Vegas, it is always better for women to have escorts. We were sitting at the Thunderbird Hotel watching the fabulous Frances Faye, when a drunken man came over to our table and asked Betty to dance. She declined politely and he went away for a while, suddenly

Top. Jack Buchanan being greedy in 'As Long As They're Happy'. (1954)
Bottom. Me being greedy.

returning even more intoxicated. On being refused a dance again, he started slanging Betty, calling her all the usual sorts of insults one expects from a drunk. Steve, one of our escorts stood up and asked him to leave us alone, and without any word of warning the man punched him in the nose and ran off leaving the poor fellow on the floor with blood pouring from his face. Betty screamed and pandemonium broke out, sheriffs appeared from all sides, and of course we were the centre of attraction. We had to take Steve to hospital, and Betty was genuinely very upset, as I do not think she had ever been involved in such a thing before and was worried that it would hit the papers. One can imagine the headlines — 'Diana Dors and Betty Grable in bar-room brawl with three men,' etc. etc. Thankfully it did not make the headlines, and sadly that was the last time I ever saw her. Somehow I will never be able to believe she is gone, those beautiful legs and the pin-up blonde looks, still dancing and dazzling when they show her old wartime movies on the television screen. Betty Grable was a star, and there will never be another like her. When she went they destroyed the mould!

G is for GREED

I suppose we are all guilty of this deadly sin at some time or other in our lives.

Probably the biggest example of mass hysteria and greed can be seen at sales time in the big department stores. Women who usually behave like perfectly normal human beings are suddenly transformed into screaming, clawing monsters ready to battle, punch or kill if necessary the first person to try and stop them from picking up a bargain, which in reality has sometimes only been knocked down slightly.

The psychology of dealing with people and their instinctive greed was once explained to me by a prominent northern showman named Jimmy Brennan who owned, amongst other things, the Queen's Theatre in Blackpool.

Back in the early fifties a young man had just made a big hit with his record of 'Oh Mein Papa', namely Eddie Calvert, the 'Man with the Golden Trumpet' as he was then billed. Jimmy Brennan badly wanted Eddie for the Blackpool summer season that year knowing he was 'hot', and would do fantastic business at his theatre. To use Jimmy's words, 'I went down to London where he was appearing at the Finsbury Park Empire determined to get him. In fact I would have been prepared to pay him a thousand pounds a week at that time, but of course being a business man, I wasn't going to let *him* know that, and would try to get him for as little as I could.'

. The unsuspecting Eddie Calvert received Jimmy Brennan in his dressing room backstage, where the wily showman in brisk and businesslike fashion, proceeded to tell him how good it would be for his career to do a season in Blackpool. 'Now then Eddie,' he went on after the initial seeds had been sown, 'I'm going to be quite honest with you about the money. I'll pay you a *hundred* pounds a week, not a penny more, because I can't afford it. Before you make up your mind I'm going to give you a chance to think it over. I'll nip off for a drink, and when I come back you can give me your answer. Remember I'm a man of my word. A hundred pounds it is, and don't bother wasting your time trying to make it a hundred and fifty.' With that he left the flabbergasted Eddie before he had time to say 'yes' or 'no'. 'Naturally I knew he wouldn't accept that offer if I had made it straight,' continued Jimmy as he related the story to me. 'So I did a bit of psychology on him, and left him to stew for about half an hour. When I returned I rushed through the door of his room just as he was about to say "no". "Eddie", I said, *"one hundred and fifty* pounds a week was my firm offer and I'll not budge from it . . . What do you say? Take it or leave it."

Eddie Calvert did a typically human thing, he accepted immediately! No doubt thinking, as Jimmy wanted him to, that the impresario had made a mistake regarding the actual amount, and done himself for an extra fifty pounds, never knowing that it was the figure he had intended to pay all along.

H is for HOAX

Practical jokes, tricks or hoaxes have never really appealed to me, probably because if done well enough, people are often badly hurt or shocked. The old gag of pulling someone's chair away just as they are about to sit down is usually the first trick one learns at school. But this, as we all know, is an extremely dangerous thing to do for, after the laughing has stopped, the person is likely to suffer a badly damaged back as a result.

I also knew one stupid man who frightened his daughter by putting a white sheet over himself pretending to be a ghost, and his jumping out from a cupboard caused the poor girl to have a speech impediment for the rest of her life. Some jokes and pranks are fairly harmless however, as proved by Tommy Steele whose claim to being the crown prince of jokers in show business in a newspaper

With Dennis Hamilton, the greatest hoaxer of all!

serial, did not appear to have created any serious repercussions, although they must have given his victims some very anxious moments.

My first husband Dennis Hamilton was a fanatic at 'pulling people's legs'! His favourite targets were policemen. So much did he detest them that the sight of one strolling along the road apparently doing nothing, incited him to report a bad fight going on somewhere nearby. The policeman would rush excitedly off in the direction indicated, leaving Dennis helpless with laughter and crying, 'I do hate to see the police standing around doing nothing!' Another of his delights would be to stop and enquire the way to a town or destination, and tie the person up in knots with double chat whilst they desperately tried to give directions. More often than not this would end in a shouting match, with irritated people losing their tempers and Dennis driving away in a stream of abuse.

No one was safe from his hoaxes. Our long-suffering family solicitor felt the brunt of them many times, but none worse than the day when something happened to displease Dennis. In a moment of madness he rearranged the man's name, and the names of the firm he worked for, which were encased in a glass frame at his office, just outside the lift to enable clients to find out where they were heading. I cannot print the exact wording here which he wickedly spelt out by twisting the letters around, but suffice to say it was extremely obscene and the solicitor rued the day he had upset him!

The telephone was also a fund of unending joy to Dennis. Many were the evenings when he would amuse himself and friends by dialling random numbers and having incredibly funny conversations with whoever answered. Some very strange people were discovered on those calls. On one occasion a scout master actually admitted, after a lot of cross-examination by Dennis pretending to be someone in authority, that he had been interfering with several of his boy scouts, and once an entire sausage factory closed down after Dennis had convinced them he was from the Ministry of Health and was about to pay a visit, due to a grave report concerning their hygiene arrangements.

Dennis's telephone games came to an abrupt halt however, when one hoax backfired badly.

He had rung up a local police station pretending to be the victim of an assault and robbery at home, and acted the part so well, that the police hurried to the address he had given them (that of a close personal friend) somewhere in Hampstead. Upon arrival they discovered a window broken and blood on the ground which confirmed their worst fears regarding the telephone call. After climbing inside they found the unfortunate friend lying there the worse for drink in his living room, having broken the window himself earlier to gain access to his own house. It took a great deal of explanation on his part to prove he had not been attacked, or that he had wasted their time with a hoax call!

An elderly woman friend of ours who lived in the middle of the village of Bray in a pretty little cottage with a yellow front door, incurred Dennis's displeasure one evening. He rushed off at dead of night and crept back to her cottage with a tin of dark green paint. Solemnly he daubed a picture of a man's genitals on her front door, with words stating the fact that she was known as the best 'lay' in the village! He returned home howling with laughter at the prospect of what would happen in the morning when people saw his handiwork as they waited for a bus, the stop being situated right outside her house.

See it they all did, causing the unfortunate woman an enormous amount of embarrassment plus the expense of having her door re-painted!

Not all Dennis's pranks were without reason of course. Occasionally if I wanted to arrive late at the film studios where they had previously been playing me up with inefficient calls, he would ring round a few other artistes and change their times, to what are known as 'stand bys'. This meant they did not have to show up in the early morning as arranged but wait at home until alerted, depending on how the filming was going along. Naturally, next day the entire company was thrown into chaos, and I too would be telephoned by a frantic assistant director to say that someone had played a hoax, obviously having done so on me too. Pretending outrage I would arrive two hours later at the studio, but happily having had an extra long lie in at home in bed.

Aside from Dennis who was the main source of hoaxes in my life, I have heard of many others played on people and some were extremely funny. Actor Richard Harris played an incredible hoax on a well known writer whom he knew had always fancied having an affair with a nun. Whilst in script conference with the writer, a 'nun' who was really an actress Richard had organised for the joke, arrived at the front door ostensibly collecting for some charity. Richard allowed the writer to admit her and then left them alone on a sudden pretext of having to pop out for something. This done, the 'nun' showed great interest in the elegance of the house and asked the writer, who was frothing at the mouth anyway, to show her around. This he did and of course when they reached the bedroom, the inevitable happened.

To this day the writer does not know that the whole thing was a set-up and fully believes he has achieved his ultimate ambition!

One of the funniest repeated hoaxes I ever heard occurred long before my time. The late bandleader Teddy Brown was a great prankster and had his house filled with gadgets and gimmicks of all kinds with which to amuse himself.

At parties, of which there were many, ladies would be guided, on request, to the cloakroom to 'spend a penny', and having placed themselves upon the toilet seat would suddenly leap off in horror. Teddy's pre-recorded taped voice, sounding like that of a cockney workman, would boom from the depths of nowhere, 'Oi! Look out missus. We're *working* down here!'

H is for HITLER

There is nothing very amusing which can be written or said about this evil man who was responsible for the rape of Europe, and the deaths of millions of people all over the world.

Charlie Chaplin did a brilliant comedy portrayal of him in a film entitled *The Great Dictator*, and the late Lenny Bruce also had some extremely funny material in his act about two Jewish theatrical producers who discover Adolf Schickelgruber the house painter, change his name and start him in show business. Other than this, apart from many cartoons, the memory of Hitler is a grim historical fact never to be erased.

It will seem strange to my reader therefore, that at this point I am now going to launch into a piece regarding Frank Sinatra, for the two men would normally never be

With Peter Lawford who also had nothing to do with Hitler.

mentioned in the same breath.

I have known 'Ole Blue Eyes' for twenty odd years now and found him to be a very charming man, totally unlike the image created by the press, against whom he has waged a private war throughout his career. It was whilst he was appearing at a nightclub in Lake Tahoe, where I had been invited by Peter Lawford and Sammy Davis Junior to attend a private party, that he told me a story relating to Hitler, which I found rather funny.

Sinatra is a man of very strong political views, so much so that during Franco's reign as the President of Spain, he sent a personal letter informing him that he would never stoop to returning there again, because he did not approve of the way Franco ran the country. The mode of Sinatra's correspondence did not, I am sure, give Franco the idea that it had been officially written at the Pentagon either, for in his own inimitable style, Sinatra had used many colourful adjectives.

Having launched upon an angry tirade appertaining to politicians in general, due to this Spanish tale, Frank went on to berate certain other people who did not agree with his own political beliefs, namely a well known extreme Right Wing group in Hollywood consisting of columnists Hedda Hopper and Mike Connolly, director John Ford, and actors Ward Bond and John Wayne, two of Ford's constant screen employees who appeared in almost every film he made.

'That Ward Bond,' seethed Sinatra, 'would ride around town on a motor cycle, wearing a black shirt and spouting fascism.' I smiled inwardly at this thought, for the vision of Bond, who was at the time playing an old wagon master in a television series called *Wagon Train*, looking like an aged Marlon Brando in *The Wild One* was quite amusing. 'I decided to teach him a lesson,' shouted Sinatra, who by now had worked himself up into a froth about the entire matter, and proceeded to relate a story to his captive dinner guests, regarding the time when he visited Germany long after the death of Hitler, sometime in the fifties.

Having found the spot where the Fuhrer is presumed to be buried, Sinatra in his usual way, leaving no holds barred, commissioned a photographer to accompany him there and take his picture. This was, however, to be no ordinary snapshot of an American tourist gazing at the bunker in awe, but a picture showing Sinatra's own personal feelings about Hitler, Fascism and the whole situation. 'I unzipped my flies, and had the cameraman take a shot of me pissing over the goddam bastard,' he proudly announced amidst much laughter. 'Then what did you do?' I asked realising the payoff had not yet come. 'I got the guy to blow up the picture real large,' he replied jubilantly, 'and I sent it to that Fascist sonofabitch Bond, signed . . . *Very truly yours*, Frank.'

H is for HOMOSEXUALS

Now that homosexuality is not only legalised, but apparently a good thing to cash in on as far as show business is concerned, I presume I can write with ease on the subject.

Before actors like John Inman acquired fame and fortune by portraying homosexuals on television, they were known as fairies, queens, pansies and nancy boys; only spoken of in sly whispers by the majority of people.

I have known literally hundreds in my time, and still do. There is always an abundance of 'gay' boys working in the theatre, and indeed a more amusing type of person one could not wish for. They also make marvellous friends and fans for women, particularly when famous, such as the late Judy Garland and Shirley Bassey, not to mention myself, for their adulation is undying.

I once made a film which was set in the Bayswater area of London. The producer was gay — so was my leading man, the dress designer and a couple of the character actors, to such an extent that I suggested at the time we should alter the title from whatever it was then, to *Queensway!*

Despite the recognition of homosexuality today there are many stars who are not known to the general public as

Left. Me in drag. *Right.* With George Gobel in 'I Marrried A Woman'.

homosexuals, and when asked by eager women about certain 'he-men' I have never had the heart to tell them the truth and spoil their illusions. Some manage to conduct their private lives quietly and with dignity, and some pretend that they are actually normal; which to my mind is hypocrisy. Indeed there was one old and well known radio star now passed on, beloved by millions and married too, who regularly made passes at a very gay friend of mine when they appeared in a theatrical revue years ago, encouraging him to sit on his lap in the dressing room!

There are of course the unfortunates like actor Peter Wyngarde who fell from favour and destroyed his public image by being indiscreet on one occasion, which resulted in a court case.

In days gone by, the brilliant Oscar Wilde was pilloried and sent to prison for two years because of his homosexual behaviour, and before the bill legalising it all was passed, as recently as 1954, Lord Montagu of Beaulieu was also imprisoned for an offence.

When I first started in films, and was placed under contract to the Rank Organisation, a film director named Brian Desmond Hurst was very prominent in the industry. Brian was, and still is, one of the most colourful characters I have ever met. He lived in great splendour amidst wealth inherited from his Irish ancestors with, amongst other things, carved wooden saints around his bedhead, and stained glass windows depicting religious scenes in the bedroom, for he was a devout Catholic. His conversation was always spiced with acid witticisms, and his impersonation of Queen Victoria on the lavatory, with a small handkerchief spread over the top of the head, and cheeks blown out to an absurd size, was unsurpassed, and famous throughout show business.

But the time I met him his sexual activities, whatever they were, were probably long finished for all I know, but he always had a penchant for beautiful boys, loving to have them around all the time. Brian always insisted that in order to gain his favour, *everybody* must be 'pretty, witty or rich'! His desire for wanting to see only the good-looking people in life was so great, that once whilst having Sunday lunch at the famous Skindles Hotel at Maidenhead, with his usual crowd of pretty boys around him, an ordinary, somewhat ugly couple walked past the table with their one year old offspring, and the sight roused him to such anger he snarled, 'Just look at those two. How dare they have the effrontery to reproduce themselves!'

Brian's social gatherings were always amusing, and inevitably one could be sure of a great deal of enjoyment at his home. One summer afternoon whilst we were all sipping champagne, he drew my attention to a young labourer who was working outside his window on some building task or other, and had apparently been doing so for some time much to Brian's delight, as he was stripped to the waist and sported a beautiful brown chest above his tightly fitting jeans. 'Go and get him,' ordered the wicked old rogue to one of his minions, and the boy was ceremoniously ushered into his elegant drawing room. Offering him a glass of bubbly, and quite oblivious of his total confusion as to why he had been hauled in there at all, Brian waited until he had drunk the champagne and remarked lecherously, his eyes fixed on the lower half of the boy's anatomy, 'Right, we've all seen what you have on display in the shop window, now let's find out what you've got at the back of the store!'

J. Arthur Rank, who we were all working for at the time, was a strict Methodist, aside from being a millionaire, and everyone connected with his organisation was expected to behave in a respectable manner. As he did not approve of alcohol, at no time were any of us permitted to be photographed with a drink in hand, not even lemonade, in case it looked like the real thing. Mr Rank made it a policy in those days to invite various producers and directors down to his country seat sometimes for the weekend. This was officially a social invitation, but unofficially it was really done so that he could give them a concentrated 'going over' so to speak, and find out if they were fit to belong to his vast empire. No one dared refuse the offer, but none really relished it, as life at J. Arthur's home was austere and hardly anybody's idea of a swinging weekend!

Eventually Brian Desmond Hurst received his instructions to attend the great man's house, and off he went in his usual merry way. Things proceeded fairly smoothly considering the difference in their two personalities, but it was during a stroll around the rose garden after dinner that J. Arthur Rank looked loftily down at Brian as he trotted beside him, saying quietly, 'Mr Hurst, I hear some rather disturbing things about your private life.' Brian gazed up at his boss and sighed with the expression of an innocent cherub, 'Sir, I am as *God* made me!'

H is for HELL

There is probably no hell for artistes in the next world. They have suffered enough from critics in this!

I is for INFIDELITY

Infidelity which is so very often the cause of divorce, should not be confused with incompatibility, also the cause of divorce! Incompatibility, aside from the obvious, is a word used often by lawyers in America, when it comes to finding a good excuse for parting two people legally, as in the case of film stars who do not wish to endure a load of mud slinging publicity. Rock Hudson and his advisors found it a useful word in court, when his 'studio arranged' marriage with a lady named Phyllis, who had once been his secretary, finally ground to an absurd halt one year after the wedding nuptials. The marriage was fixed to make Rock look more like a 'he-man' for his fans, and although I attended the anniversary party in Hollywood along with hundreds of other stars, and witnessed the pair posing lovingly over the swimming pool, where their names were spelt out in dark red roses, how were we all to know that a few weeks later, when the publicity machines had finished spewing out syrup on the Hudsons, divorce headlines with words like 'incompatibility' would be flying around for everyone to hear.

Having now written about the subject of incompatibility, I will revert to what this piece is supposed to be all about, namely infidelity. Most married men are guilty of this during their lives, but then they must also have a woman to help them! Kings, presidents, rich men, poor men, they all seem to get up to a bit of extra-marital hanky panky at some time or other. It is very easy to indulge in scandal about people after they are dead, but even when alive, rumours flowed rife through Hollywood regarding the behaviour of the late John Kennedy, and his younger brother Bobby. I actually witnessed the latter practically seducing some young actress in a darkened corner of Ciro's nightclub on Sunset Strip where I was appearing in cabaret in 1960, to such a degree that I do not believe he even saw *my* performance at all that night, so intent was he on his own. Now, of course, rumours of his relationship with Marilyn Monroe circulate wildly, and who is to say whether or not they are ture, of if Ethel and Jackie, the

With a midnight cowboy in 'The Unholy Wife'. Hollywood 1956.

long-suffering wives of he and President Kennedy, were as unhappy and shocked by their husbands' infidelities as any other women would have been.

Frank Sinatra, no stranger to the world of infidelity amongst married men, publicly denounced John Kennedy as his friend and political ally, for whom he had done much during his campaign to elect him into the White House. The reason for this outburst was because a certain Hollywood actress (now an enormously big star with her own series on television and whom Sinatra had introduced to Kennedy in the first place) went to stay with the President, on his instructions, at Bing Crosby's luxury home in Palm Springs for a swinging weekend. This was taken as a direct rebuff by Sinatra, who wished them to make their love nest at his own palatial home there. Thoroughly miffed by the entire episode, he even dismissed the film actor Peter Lawford from his famous 'Clan' blaming him for the whole incident. Lawford was the President's brother-in-law at the time and, according to the gospel of

Sinatra, should have influenced and advised Kennedy to be loyal! So much for infidelity amongst politicians and film stars, but what about behaviour in ordinary suburbia?

During my travels around England, I have never ceased to be surprised at what goes on between married couples. Many times in the middle of my cabaret act in some remote borough or city, I would remark that I had read about this sort of thing in the *News of the World*, but never believed it actually happened!

One of the first occasions I discovered infidelity in the outer suburbs was at a peaceful country spot somewhere up North. During the week that I was appearing in an exclusive country club there, my manager and I became quite friendly with some of the local folk, who all seemed harmless and quiet enough on the surface, aside from the fact that they probably drank too much. There were the usual couples, the doctor and his wife, the coal merchant and his, etc. etc. and after my opening night we were invited back to one of their lovely country homes for drinks. This was all very convivial, dancing to the record player, refreshments brought out at two a.m. and of course plenty more drinking. I perceived my manager getting along extremely well with a couple of the wives, and I too was being flattered and complimented by several husbands due, I thought, to the fact that I was a famous name and everyone was excited to see me there. A few more nights of this sort of revelry followed, and more and more 'locals' kept arriving to join in the fun! Finally, having been invited to an old world thatched cottage after the show one evening, it dawned on me what was happening. Everyone was swapping partners! And it was becoming quite apparent that my manager and I were the prizes for the end of the week! No doubt they were all looking forward to it immensely, having softened us up so well with hospitality. At the moment I realised this fact, I was just climbing into the car of a well known MP who was playing host for the night. My manager had been captured by the MP's wife in her car and was quite oblivious of it all, so thrilled was he to be making such remarkable headway with all the local females. A situation he was totally unused to I might add. Amidst the noise of excited husbands revving up their engines ready to drive off with whichever wife they had landed, like so many fishermen with their hauls, my own host who was obviously hoping to get me back to the thatched cottage on his own, suddenly slammed on the brakes and got out of the car. 'What are you doing?' I asked nervously as he peered anxiously at the vehicle ahead of us where his wife was revving up her own engine, my unsuspecting manager at her side. 'Oh thank God for that,' he sighed stepping back into the car and preparing to make off with me at last. 'As long as my wife has got herself a man, we can all relax!' I hasten to explain to my reader, that despite his wife's infidelity, there was one very disappointed MP in a small corner of England that night, as I hastily beat it back to my hotel.

Pop star P. J. Proby is one of the most paranoid men I know regarding infidelity. Married three times, and with hundreds of affairs behind him, he mistrusts every woman he knows, presumably due to some disastrous incident in his extreme youth. His last wife Dulcie, an ex-Blackpool card dealer, suffered the worst at his hands, probably because having reached forty, and now an alcoholic, he is completely paranoid about unfaithful women.

One evening a few nights after being fired from the hit show *Elvis* in which he had made a marvellous comeback, he and Dulcie, fortified with too much bourbon, came to visit my husband and me, at our home in Berkshire. Not being good at staying up late I finally went to bed at around two thirty a.m. leaving Alan to cope with their drunken ramblings, which by now had become rather tedious. I was awakened from my sleep a few hours later by an hysterical Dulcie clutching the bedpost, and pleading with me to help her calm Proby down. 'He's gone mad and punched me in the eye,' she wailed miserably.

During the night he had passed out on the sofa with my Siamese cat at his feet. Alan had then been bored to death by Dulcie who, between massive gulps of bourbon, proceeded to tell him the story of her life. Suddenly Proby awoke, his cowboy hat back to front and looking rather like Gabby Hayes. 'I have woken up to infidelity', he roared. 'There has been infidelity goin' on here.' Alan, a man who is quick to lose his temper, immediately retaliated hotly, 'Are you insinuating that I have had an affair with your wife whilst you have been asleep?' 'I'm not insinuating anything,' replied Proby, now squaring up to the unfortunate Dulcie, fists clenched, 'But she is a whore.' Alan grabbed him as he took his first swing at her. 'Well who the hell is she supposed to have had an affair with then? Diana is upstairs asleep, and the cat has been doctored, so that leaves *me*,' he raged. 'I'm not accusing you, but she is a whore,' persisted Proby breaking free from Alan's grasp and landing one on his wife's nose. Appalled at the sight of a man striking a woman, Alan punched him across the living room, and as he slid down the wall cowboy hat still askew. 'Congratulations! I concede defeat.' Proby cried, 'you are the first man ever to put me on my arse.' Defeated or not, a few days later when mercifully they had left our home, Dulcie was obviously accused of infidelity again, and the entire affair ended with Proby accidentally shooting her, necessitating hospitalisation.

The most idiotic piece of infidelity I have ever known was not connected with the drunken carryings-on of the Probys however.

Another pop star, this time British, was having a very heavy affair with one of identical twin sisters. In those far off days he had not yet made it in the music world, or anywhere else for that matter, and was forced to live in a small room with his wife in Paddington. The twins who were in show business themselves, had also fallen on hard times, and during a mad moment, he invited them both to live with he and his wife sharing their sparse accommodation. It goes without saying that the twin with whom he was having the affair must have been insane to accept such an offer, but accept she did! Had it been more than a bed sit things might have been more agreeable, but the sleeping arrangements in one room were such, that the twins had a makeshift bed at one end, and the husband and wife on a let-down settee at the other.

Life went fairly smoothly, with the wife blissfully unaware of the affair taking place between her husband and his girlfriend every time she popped out for the groceries, but things were not so easy at night for him when she insisted on her conjugal rights, and he was forced to perform what he termed as his duty! The twin laying awake in the other bed whilst her sister slumbered happily, seethed with jealousy as she heard him desperately trying to make love as quietly as possible without her knowledge, something which he denied vehemently each time she challenged him about it in the daytime. Eventually she could stand it no longer and broke off the affair, angrily accusing him of deliberate infidelity with his own wife!

I is for INCEST

The word itself has a pretty nasty sound, but then its context is also very unsavoury. Incest is still something which even in this day and age is talked about in a whisper, and unlike homosexuality or abortion which have been legalised in many cases, it is a subject, or should I say pastime, which is not permitted or recognised by society.

I have known a few girls who in their teens were mildly interfered with by their fathers, and although I was appalled, it seemed much better than a mother who actually allows her son to perform a sexual deed. This is no doubt due to the fact that I consider men to be more foolish than women where sex is concerned, and have often witnessed fathers having a sly cuddle and grope with their daughters on the pretext of being a loving parent, when all they were really doing was getting a cheap thrill!

The mother and son syndrome is a totally different matter. I once knew a man who regularly had sexual intercourse with his mother. His explanation that she was a nymphomaniac who had been married four times into the bargain, never really appeased the horrible picture I envisaged of the pair of them in the act of sex, and it did not do him much good psychologically either, as aside from the perverted effect on his youth, he proceeded to marry no less than six women as the years went by, and will more than likely do it a few times again before he is finished.

A film producer I knew, had a mother who was so besotted with him, that her jealousy overcame her when he eventually brought home the girl he intended to marry. The wedding ceremony went off without a hitch, his mother managing to control her emotions well enough throughout, but at the reception later in his flat she began falling apart, and made scathing remarks to her unfortunate new daughter-in-law. Finally, unable to contain herself any further, she leapt into the honeymoon bed just as we all began saying our goodbyes, in order to allow the bridal couple to be by themselves at last. I do not know how long it took the groom to persuade her to emerge from between the sheets, but I gather he only managed to extract her after solemnly promising that she could remain in the flat with them, and not go home alone. The wretched woman then spent the night with her ear to their bedroom keyhole, which cannot have been very comfortable for the bride, so it was hardly surprising that the marriage foundered very quickly afterwards and ended in divorce, much to his mother's delight!

As a last note on this rather sordid subject, sexual practice also seems to be common with in-laws. To most men the idea of having sex with their mother-in-law would be utterly repellent and unthinkable, but I know one man who does so twice a year! The actual dates are not significant. In other words they do not keep their love trysts at Christmas or August bank holiday for instance. Before anyone starts sighing about deep emotions, and 'love knowing no bounds', I must state that love does *not* enter into their situation. The lady is extremely wealthy and fancies her son-in-law, he in turn adores jewellery, and so whenever I see him sporting a new Cartier watch or some other such valuable trinket, I know he has been round on a 'duty call' to his mother-in-law again.

With my son Jason and Violet-Elizabeth in 'Just William'.

I is for INCOME TAX

My own terrible battles with the Inland Revenue have been publicised in detail like those of many other unfortunate folk in show business!

No one enjoys paying the Income Tax man his dues but of course it is a rigidly enforced rule that all must do so! Those who do not are hunted down and captured, and often end up in the bankruptcy court.

I have three sons, Mark, Gary and Jason. Mark and Jason would never qualify for any 'scholar of the year award', although both are exceptionally bright, until of course it comes to getting down to the ordinary business of studying.

Mark is, at the time of writing, eighteen years old, living in Hollywood, and despite his singularly unspectacular years at school, progressing in life extremely well. At the tender age of six however, on hearing of my impending bankruptcy, he suddenly came up with a scheme one day which did have a hint of genius about it, although unfortunately I did not follow it through. 'I know how you could solve your Income Tax problem,' he announced happily, as if any fool could have worked it out, even me. 'Simply do as the Beatles did. Form a company which owns *you*, and let them deal with it!'

Sadly my eldest son did not become an accountant after this sound piece of advice, and as is probably known, I went bankrupt!

As the years went by, with correspondence arriving from the Tax authorities every morning in the mail, my youngest son Jason also became aware of my constant battle with the tax man, and seethed angrily for me when he saw how upset I became about the whole matter. Apart from these moments at the breakfast table, I did not imagine he remembered any of it, until one day I was driving him to the rehearsals of the television series *Just William* in which I played Mrs Bott, and Jason had been given a tiny part as a member of William's gang.

On passing the Houses of Parliament he suddenly shouted, 'Quick Mummy, get down,' in such a warning voice it nearly caused me to swerve the car, 'What for?' I demanded, trying to recover my equilibrium. Solemnly pointing to a window in that dignified building, my seven year old 'boy wonder' replied, 'So that the tax man does not see you driving past in a Rolls Royce!'

J is for JITTERBUGGING

This really dates me, and no doubt younger readers will wonder what the hell I am talking about, but in my youth *this* was the method of dancing, and giving vent to one's feelings on the dance floor, to the sounds of the big bands. It started in America of course, and like all other dance crazes went the way of the Big Apple, The Twist, and all the rest.

It is a sure sign of age when one wistfully looks at young people saying that 'we never had it so good in our day', but honestly, we didn't! Today kids can shake, rattle, roll and wriggle all by themselves, and generally 'do their thing' without fear of intrusion, but when I first started going to dances there were large forbidding signs placed sternly everywhere with the words, 'No Jitterbugging Allowed', as if it were some sort of criminal act, and if one persisted in a corner just craftily dancing the dreaded 'jitterbug', then one would be firmly shown the door.

Actually the summing up of today's dancing was done perfectly by authoress Mary Hayley Bell, mother of Hayley Mills, and wife of John; who said at a party one night, having flopped down exhausted from a session on the dance floor, 'How I long for the old days when one was swept away in someone's arms! Now all they do is stand there shaking by themselves, one might just as well masturbate!'

J is for JOCASTA
This is a role any actress would give her eye teeth for, and one which I am delighted to say I played at the Chichester

After the crab was over.

Theatre, in a production of *Oedipus*.

Jocasta is the only woman in the entire play, and I was able to go to town with the make-up, wearing sparkles on my face, a magenta coloured wig set in strange little plaits, and exotic clothes and jewellery. The men wore fabulous brass necklaces, covered themselves in thick body make-up from head to foot, shaved their heads, and were clothed in rainbow coloured robes. All in all, a highly spectacular and colourful affair.

I often wonder whether the public have any idea of what goes on behind the scenes, without the glamour of the stage production. The dingy dressing-rooms and back-stages of most theatres are pretty gloomy and more often than not, very dirty too, although not so in the case of Chichester.

Usually when a play has settled down to a comfortable run, the actors allow their tensions to ease up, and it is very amusing to see them rush sometimes from a game of cards, in order to cope perhaps with a highly emotional scene. The audience sitting enraptured, occasionally in tears, little realise that only minutes before they had been doing something quite mundane!

Such was the case one night at Chichester. Comedy actor Alfred Marks looked magnificent in his make-up and brass jewellery as Creon, my brother, in the play. Five minutes before going on stage to be dethroned by Oedipus, a very powerful scene, he came rushing into my dressing-room with a highly delectable crab he had purchased that day down by the seashore. Alfred is a gourmet and excitedly showed me his shellfish, asking if I knew how to prepare it. 'No, I'm sorry I don't', I answered, feeling a bit foolish, for I supposed *everyone* but me knew how to get a crab ready for consumption. 'I'll show you,' he said hurriedly, as his cue was within minutes of approaching. So saying, he ran off and reappeared a moment later with a hammer. 'What the hell are you doing with that?' I asked nervously; for in his warlike costume he looked as if he was going to do some nasty damage. 'Just watch and I'll show you how to get the best pieces out of the bloody thing,' he said, and without further ado began smashing the crab all over my dressing table, sampling bits of the flesh with relish. The whole scene was totally bizarre, for there was Alfed dressed as the pagan Creon, me as Jocasta, noisily hammering at a crab, and grabbing bits of it to eat, as though we had been starving for a month! 'If only the audience could see us now . . . they would never

Working with Alfred was great fun during that production. A typical example of his humour happened at the dress rehearsal, for having described the colourful

112

jewellery and dramatic costumes worn by the men, to my reader, I shrieked with laughter when Alfred, clad exotically in red robe and earrings, strolled into my room covered in dark brown body make-up, and said, 'I'm just going down to the fish and chip shop, shall I bring you back a bit of cod?'

J is for JAMES ROBERTSON JUSTICE

The late blustery, bearded actor, who once taught me how to eat oysters, in a slightly different way from Alfred Marks' crab lesson, and whose acid wit in the film world was one which made many a producer shudder if James did not like him. James was never afraid of speaking his mind, in fact he revelled in it, and thoroughly enjoyed cutting people down to size if they became too stroppy. Years ago,

With James and other stars at the Venice Film Festival, 1955.

he played my millionaire father in a film entitled *An Alligator Named Daisy* and romped about the fabulous sets with glee, lording it over everyone as if he really were worth millions!

James's (no one ever dared to call him Jimmy) stock went higher than ever amongst the film folk during the filming of *Alligator*, when he brought his old friend and naval colleague Prince Philip down to Pinewood Studios one day and 'showed him the ropes', as he put it.

One unfortunate incident did occur whilst we were making the film however. James asked if he could come and stay at my house in Bray for the night, as he was unable to get back to his home in Hampshire and be at the studios again early the next morning. I say 'unfortunate' because I had a married couple staying there at the time, whose constant violent quarrelling was famous throughout showbusiness, and I was forced to put him in a bedroom right next door to the battling pair. Their rantings and ravings lasted most of the night, and poor James got no sleep at all due to the noise, thus arriving at the studios the following morning more exhausted than if he had driven up from Hampshire. Apologising profusely, I suggested he should perhaps come and live on the river, for I was anxious to reassure him that on normal occasions, life there was very peaceful, besides the convenience of being near film studios. 'What', he thundered, 'live on the Thames? *Never* . . . it's full of stockbrokers in electric canoes!'

K is for KU KLUX KLAN

I suppose now that I am a Catholic convert I too would come under the wrath and vengeance this group hand out to those who do not conform to their idea of respectable Christian behaviour.

If my information is correct, and I have not really studied the situation very much, as happily the Klan is not formed here in England, they are against Catholics, Jews and Negroes. The Negro seems to be the worst hit however, as in the Southern States of America there are many more of them than Jews or Catholics.

In the last few years the vogue for family sagas on television has increased, and one of the most successful was *Roots*, the story of a negro sold into slavery, his subsequent adventures, and the descendants who were all plunged into one tragedy following another until the entire plot became unbearable!

It was probably a sick joke, but the story went around inside show business circles that the Ku Klux Klan had bought the film rights of *Roots*, and were planning to show it backwards so that it would have a happy ending!

K is for KNIGHT

The fairy tale myth of the knight in shining armour who rescues the princess from the jaws of the dragon and carries her off on his white horse, has been well and truly exploded in this age we live in. Certainly many a poor unsuspecting female, including myself, weaned on the idea of finding her hero and living 'happily ever after', has suffered the experience of finding out that all this childhood propaganda was really a *myth* in the true sense of the word.

Probably the only knights of any consequence we are aware of are the Knights of the theatre. This brings me immediately to my theory, and it is one shared by many fellow artistes, that actors should not be given titles, for we are all basically 'strolling players'. Gypsies, vagabonds, and in some cases thieves!

The late actor Henry Irving, first to be knighted a 'Sir', was really to blame for starting it all. One of his contemporaries moaned bitterly at the time, 'Henry should never have accepted the knighthood, he has made us all respectable.' However, it has gone on from there, and now we have so many theatrical Knights, it has become almost farcical!

With Harry H. Corbett in 'Steptoe Rides Again'. So far he has only got an O.B.E.

It is of course a great honour, awarded presumably for an actor's ability to do what is really only a job of work, and who is to say which selected few should be singled out from others who are all equally as good? Perhaps I would not feel so strongly about it if the powers that be offered to make me a 'Dame', but God forbid the day will ever come. I would hate that title anyway, it reminds me of Old Mother Riley!

Dame Diana Dors has a pantomime ring to it and is not nearly as dignified as say, Sir Michael Redgrave, or even more illustrious, Lord Olivier. I am not knocking any of the noble theatrical Knights, neither am I undermining their talents, though I suspect that deep down beneath those lofty exteriors, there must lurk some very satisfied egos at being dubbed with a title above all the rest. However, who am I to say that Sir Ralph Richardson, Sir John Mills, Sir Richard Attenborough, etc, do not warrant the odd curtsey as a result of their labours. The pleasure they must derive from their honours is probably summed up by the sweet little tale of Sir John Gielgud who was once placed in the terrible position of trying to board a bus in Sloane Square, no doubt after a performance at the Royal Court Theatre where he has had so many triumphs. Sadly Sir John's judgement as to where the platform actually was, seems to have been slightly impaired that day, and one of his noble feet got caught in a position which prevented him from either boarding or disembarking. In this undignified and dangerous state he was forcibly carried around the square, apparently to the complete indifference of the driver and passengers who, with all due respect, did not appear to even recognise him.

Thinking his end was in sight, with, much worse, not even a good round of applause to 'go out on', the poor man swallowed his pride and called out in frantic desperation, ennunciating in the clear Shakespearian tones which had helped to earn him his Knighthood . . . 'Stop, stop. You are killing a *genius!*'

K is for KRAY

The very name, said one author, is synonymous with violence and evil. I am sorry but I do not agree. The notorious Kray twins Ronnie and Reggie, were accused of gangland crimes, and sentenced to life imprisonment. It is easy to kick people when they are down, and much of the backbiting which goes on even now in the underworld where they once operated, is jealousy on the part of their lesser contemporaries.

I do not uphold any of the wrongs which occurred during their reign, but when it comes to justice, I think they were given a rough deal!

Besides doing a great deal of marvellous work for charities, the Kray twins always remained totally within their own business, whatever it was. Since their absence, London is no longer a safe place to walk around, even in daylight, where once crime was kept in control by their tough empire. And if the Krays did worse than mugging

117

old ladies, and battering little children to death, for which most of the guilty now receive ridiculously lenient sentences, then let the people who condemn them stand up and be proven right.

L is for LIBRA

Without doubt the most argumentative men in the world are born under this sign, and I should know for my father was the first Libran I ever knew. These men are always quite convinced they are *right* in everything, even when proved wrong — but other than that it is a very artistic, romantic sign, and Libran women are extremely capable and efficient in whatever they do — I know this for I am nearly one myself, born just on the cusp of Libra and Scorpio. Sadly the Scorpio side got the better of me!

L is for LOCATION

'Beware of the dangers of a summer romance,' warn all the experts when young girls start thinking of their seaside holidays. The same can certainly be said for a love affair which begins whilst on location for a film. Suddenly a group of people combining good looks, talent, and skill at their craft, are thrown together in what is very often a 'paradise' spot, and forced to live and work for weeks at a time, whilst trying to resist the temptations of the flesh.

On most locations, almost like troops in battle and far away from home, film folk tend to behave in a completely different manner from the way they do normally, and as the time goes by one sees various couples gradually getting together, i.e. the cameraman with the wardrobe mistress, the boom operator with the continuity girl and so on.

My first film location after arriving in Hollywood was a riot. It was in the beautiful vineyard country of the Nappa

Valley, California, and the director was notorious for his love of ladies, namely the late John Farrow, father of Mia. I had a stand-in named Dee who bore a striking resemblance to Marilyn Monroe, and naturally every man on the film was after her, not the least of these was of course 'Fearless Farrow' himself, who made it his nightly pilrimage to walk around the motel where we were all ensconced, peering in at the windows and trying to find out who was making it with Dee.

After several frustrating nocturnal trips, he found her in the arms of the second assistant director, and with a shout of triumph carried her off to his own room!

This would not really have been so bad, but for the fact that 'Fearless' was a staunch Catholic (married to the long suffering Maureen O'Sullivan), and had written many books on the subject, which made him believe, in his exuberance about religion, that he had his own private staircase up to heaven.

The following morning, having enjoyed the delights of Dee, he dragged her to Mass, and made her confess all she had done, not only with him, but the rest of the unit too!

Location-style fun and games do go on in film studios as well of course. During the lunchtime break, many a dressing room has been the place for sizzling love making sessions by the film's co-stars, who also linger there after the day's work is done, loath to return home to their respective spouses. Passionate emotions have also run riot in portable dressing room trailers on the set itself, with tired technicians turning a blind eye! In the case of Hollywood star Mamie Van Doren (one of the competitors for my sex symbol crown back in the fifties), this was a somewhat difficult task, as her trailer would literally rock from side to side throughout lunch!

On location naturally things are easier, and much more private, for anyone who wishes to indulge in a bit of flirtation while the going is good. The stars themselves have the privacy of their hotel suites, with no prying eyes to worry about, or Mamie, shaking trailers!

Sanctuary in the location hotel suite was not quite so private on one occasion however, for the late King of

119

Hollywood, Clark Gable. A young British actor was making his debut with the great screen idol, and several screen goddesses, herded together in the traditional way, somewhere in the wilds of Africa. The actor discovered that the hotel accommodation, which up till then had been a row of tents out in the bush, and singularly non-private with all the lovemaking going on after nightfall, consisted of an identical group of buildings in close proximity, almost like a cell block.

One evening after filming was done, he indulged in some rather heavy drinking, and eventually at bedtime staggered towards his room in the hotel. One can only imagine that the African locking system was extremely faulty, for having drifted down what appeared to be his corridor, he flung open the door rather noisily, and to his immediate horror came face to face with the 'king', at that moment caught in the act of making love to one of his leading ladies.

The only location I ever got was a bed or a sofa.

'I say, I'm most frightfully sorry,' he stammered help-lessly, rooted to the spot with fear and embarrassment, 'I thought this was *my* room.'

'Get out,' ordered the King angrily, and needing no second bidding the unfortunate actor fled shamefacedly from the room.

What the leading lady felt at being found in such a compromising position no one will ever know. But as time went by and the actor himself became a star, he was able to relate the tale with more humour, the way he told it to me. One thing was sure however, he did not receive an invitation to her regal wedding which took place some years later, and in keeping with the outwardly 'cool' exterior she always displayed, she did not deign to send one to the King either!

L is for LUST

This is a beautiful sounding word, sexy, earthy, and used mainly to describe men's feelings for women! i.e. actor Omar Sharif's confession that as soon as he spied Barbra Streisand, his co-star in the film they made together, he 'lusted after her', and all the more credit to him for openly saying what he felt, instead of leching in a quiet and rather obscene manner, the way many men do.

By the same token, a singer may be described as having a 'lusty' pair of lungs, and what other description can be more fitting for the fabulous dusky songstress Shirley Bassey. Aside from Tom Jones, and he is a male anyway, I cannot think of another person who belts out a song the way Shirley does, and it is, whilst on the subject of the Tiger Bay Tigress, that I now relate this lustful little story.

During my career I have had many managers, but none so amusing as one named Tony Lewis, who has accompanied most stars around the world besides myself, and on this occasion was doing the same with Shirley, in Manila. As was his way, Tony stood in the wings one evening whilst she performed her act to a packed house,

The director said, 'Look lustful'. 'Tread Softly Stranger'. (1958)

accompanied by the brilliant pianist Kenny Clayton.

Looking through the curtains, Tony, who always had an eye for a lovely girl, saw what he described as the most beautiful and ravishing thing he had ever seen in his life, sitting three rows back with another girl. Never one to let an opportunity pass, Tony managed somehow to catch her attention, and during the next thirty minutes, or what was left of Shirley's act, conveyed the fact by various signals, that he would like to meet her after the show, at the hotel where he was staying.

La Bassey, also quick to observe situations, rushed off stage afterwards and excitedly said: 'Did you see that gorgeous girl?' to which of course Tony was happy to reply that he had. Not only that, but she and her friend were also lined up for a date with him and pianist Kenny later.

To his delight, at the arranged time, the two girls arrived, and he and Kenny proceeded to entertain them with dinner and drinks. Eventually as the night began to wane, they both succeeded in manoeuvring them back to their respective rooms, and Tony looked forward, with something which can only be described as out and out lust, to making love to this exquisite creature. The girl was not eager to rush headlong into bed however, and whilst he lay there in a frenzy of excitement, she commenced to titillate his emotions even further by performing a strip, combined with a sexy little dance, as only, one imagines, a Manilan lady can do.

As she slowly peeled off her clothing, and revealed the most perfect body he had ever seen, still discreetly hiding parts of it with tiny pink bra and panties, Tony, who had been going along with the dance routine, thinking it might be some sort of 'pre-lovemaking custom' out there, could contain himself no longer!

His sexual passion aroused to fever pitch, and his desire out of control, he made a lunge in her direction as she swayed provocatively near him, and lustfully grabbed at the seat of her panties.

To his ultimate horror, the beautiful maiden from Manila revealed in that moment of lust and ecstasy that She was in fact a He!

Cold sweat pouring down his face, and instantly reduced to a shrivelled wreck, Tony fell back on the bed unable to believe his bad luck, but the 'girl' was not to be put off so easily, and proceeded to offer a performance for no money at all, which was her usual custom, as she had taken a genuine fancy to him!

At length after a great deal of arguing, he managed to persuade his 'date' to get dressed and leave, though it was difficult to convey in another language that he had not realised all along it was a boy! As he opened his bedroom door sighing with relief, and shoving the protesting 'female' through it, the door of the opposite bedroom opened at precisely the same moment, and Kenny Clayton appeared with *his* lady of the evening, looking amazed . . . 'Hey, guess what?' he started to say. But to his chagrin, Tony already knew the dreadful truth.

The story, like most others, did have a somewhat amusing ending however. Singer Matt Munro, who was also appearing in Manila, stopped a rather dejected Tony in the hotel lobby the very next day and enquired who the devastatingly beautiful girl was he had seen him with the previous evening. Perking up at the chance of a joke as always, Tony informed poor Matt where she could be contacted, and suggested he invite her to the hotel for some cocktails.

Upon his return to England, Tony received a call from Matt's wife asking in rather irate tones what he was up to out there, as she had not had a letter from him for some time. 'I hope he is behaving himself,' she said suspiciously. 'Oh yes,' replied Tony innocently, 'the last time I heard of him, he was having drinks at the hotel bar with a fellow!'

M is for MARRIED MEN

Heaven help the poor unsuspecting female who becomes involved with one of these, in my opinion the most deadly type of male, and there are millions of them. If I sound as though I am speaking from bitter experience, it is probably because I am, although thankfully, my experiences have been short though sour!

My first married man was an actor in his late thirties, which seemed very ancient to me then, as I was a mere sixteen years old at the time. He was very handsome, drove around in a white car (in those days anyone who had a car at all was unique), and completely swept me off my feet the day he found me at the film studios testing for a small part in a film he was starring in.

With two well-known married men, Dean Martin and Jerry Lewis.

I was totally in awe of him and for six months whilst he amused himself with my emotions, I went through all the traumas a girl can expect to feel when associating with a man who already has a wife. The only thing he did not do was give me the old line about her 'not really understanding him'. *I* was the one who did not understand!

She was an actress, appearing in the theatre in London's West End, and nightly he would collect me from the Y.W.C.A. where I lived, my parents considering it the only safe place for a young and innocent girl to be, take me to dinner at some smart restaurant, blow my mind with a great deal of knowledgeable humour which he had in abundance, drive me home, and rush to the theatre to pick his wife up at the end of the play.

When it all came to the inevitable, miserable halt, with me heart-broken, I vowed I would never become entangled with a married man again! I did of course, but managed to escape the ordeal until I was in my early thirties.

I could write a book on the subject of men, married or

otherwise, but I will save that for another time. For the moment I am merely going to mention a few incidents which I have encountered along life's way, and trust they may benefit some women readers who so far have managed to keep married men in their place.

Men have always been a constant source of amazement to me, their behaviour patterns, infidelities, and general problems seem much greater than that of we women. I watch most of the married ones I know to this day, deceiving their wives, and running around in endless circles trying to stay young, with almost a sympathetic humour.

Once, when I was again sixteen (everything seemed to happen to me at that age) I was asked to do some private photographic modelling for a very respectable member of the London Camera Club, an establishment where I would model for amateur photographers at the esteemed fee of one guinea an hour.

Having arranged myself in a suitable pose at his flat, wearing a brief bikini, and plied by him with a few very strong gin and tonics which he had liberally poured out in anticipation of the fun he hoped would be happening after the photo session, I suddenly heard a car drive up to the front door, and a woman's voice calling out to him. Never have I seen a man go quite so ashen faced! His wife had obviously arrived home unexpectedly.

Practically falling over and smashing the camera equipment, he changed from being a suave Romeo, into a gibbering, frantic fool, rushing me into a changing room to get dressed, and bundling me out of the back door as quickly as possible. I could not really understand at the time what all the fuss was about, but now looking back, it is all crystal clear that he was an average married man up to no good.

One of the weirder things I found out about men, married or otherwise, was just after the birth of my first son Mark. For a good three months they would constantly keep asking me if I was actually feeding the baby *myself*, a question which at the time, I was quite unprepared for, and really embarrassed by. I have never thought to ask another woman if she was breast feeding her baby, it was something that did not interest me frankly, and when I reconsider the whole business now, I realise that not one woman ever bothered to ask me either.

Over the years, I have witnessed so many married men being unfaithful to their wives, it has never ceased to amaze me. As I am in show business I probably know more actors who are at it than ordinary men. Some on a serious level of course, but generally speaking 'one night stands' or sexual conquests at parties, are usually the type of thing they strive for.

Sean Connery, a frequent guest at my home for fun and games after playing golf at Wentworth, was a great stud in his time. Naturally, he was highly desired by all the ladies, as at the time he was of course James Bond, surrounded by beautiful starlets during the day on the film set, and chased by all and sundry at night.

Not that they needed to do much chasing, for Sean was always ready for any girl, a point which struck me as odd. Here was a man who could have had his pick of most women in the world, and yet, indiscriminately, at my home he would play around with any female who chanced to be there. The local barmaid, hairdresser, or just some strange girl who may have been brought along for the evening.

At this time he was also married to actress Diane Cilento, who had gone away on location in Arizona to do a film with Paul Newman, so she was hardly sitting at home waiting with his dinner in the oven. The marriage finally ended in divorce and it did not surprise me, indeed I was amazed it had lasted as long as it did under the circumstances.

Engelbert Humperdinck, another married man always ready to play when the cat was away so to speak, came violently unstuck at one point when one of his paramours sued him for a paternity suit. I often wondered how he explained that one away to his wife!

To end this distressing subject on a humorous note however, married men are also guilty of other types of horoughly naughty behaviour towards their wives. Comedy actor Jackie Smethurst who found fame in the television series *Love Thy Neighbour*, has been a friend of my husband Alan for many years. Before he hit fame and fortune though, he and his wife were living in a very nice country house with their children, and a new car which he had bought. Jackie valued his new possession highly, but one terrible day whilst driving it proudly round the neighbourhood, he accidentally bumped into another car, causing a nasty dent on the back bumper and scratching the paintwork. Terrified to tell his wife what had happened, for he had always criticised strongly the way *she* drove, he quickly put the car back in their garage and left it, whilst he went out for a drink with Alan.

Upon returning, the crafty Jackie asked his sweet and amiable wife if she would drive down to the shop to get him some cigarettes which he had forgotten. Off she went like a dutiful wife without noticing the back of the car, as he had been careful to park it in such a way that the damage could not be seen.

'Watch this,' he whispered to Alan as she returned, and on the pretext of greeting her at the door, feigned horror as he pointed to the terrible scratches and dents. 'What have you done?' he yelled accusingly. The poor woman went white. 'Oh Jackie it must have happened when I was in the shop getting your cigarettes,' she sobbed miserably. 'That's right, blame me,' stormed the culprit, using the old trick of 'attacking to defend' in a fraught situation, 'I told you to be careful with our brand new car.'

Well Mrs Smethurst, I can now reveal the truth about your husband. Happily, it is not as bad as the truth regarding most of the other married men I know!

M is for MILLION DOLLAR MOVIE

An extremely illustrious title, and misused a great deal! Originally it was thought up by American television sponsors in order to lure people into watching old films shown on late night TV there.

The first experience I had of this was many years ago whilst working in New York. My telephone kept ringing with excited agents and friends informing me I could be seen that night in the *Million Dollar Movie* slot on a particular channel. I argued that they must be mistaken, for I had never made a film that cost anywhere near that amount of money. But they insisted it was me, and that the title of the film was *Dead by Midnight*.

Confident they were all in for a big let down, I settled back at the appropriate hour to view this film, in which I was sure I had not taken part. Suddenly, I saw myself loom up on the screen in a modest little cheap budget picture, known in those days as a B film, which I had made in England quite a few years before, with actor Patrick Holt. The title of course was different. *Dead by Midnight* was much more commercial for American audiences than the original *Miss Tulip Stays the Night*, which I had never liked anyway!

Million Dollar Movie blazed the advertising blurb, whilst a soothing American voice oozed some sort of verbal warm-up as to what excitement was in store for everyone, after the various ads for washing powders and second hand cars were over.

I can only conclude that the American public were as dismayed as I was at the subsequent offering which followed, despite its impressive title, and certainly the friends who had so excitedly telephoned earlier informing me about the wretched film in the first place, did not call with congratulations the next day.

I am of course going back quite a long way in the telling of that particular story. Nowadays, films cost much more than a mere million dollars to make, and certain stars demand at least that for their personal services. This was the situation when a mammoth movie was planned, and made, in Hollywood some years back, which was to be the greatest Biblical extravaganza ever made, entitled naturally *The Greatest Story Ever Told*. It was to outdo anything Cecil B. DeMille had ever done, and aside from its obvious theme, which was about the greatest in the

With Patrick Holt in 'Dead by Midnight'.

world, namely Christ Himself, it was going to have all the greatest stars in the movie firmament playing cameos and small parts to help it along. Indeed, stars were falling over themselves to speak merely a few lines in this great film, and collect the enormous wages being paid for doing so.

Having assembled a magnificent cast of the greatest names in Hollywood to star in his production, director George Stevens wanted even more. He needed the biggest superstar he could find to play the small, but vitally important role of the centurion who stands beside the cross where Christ has died, speaking the immortal words which set the seal on the whole story: 'Truly, this man was the son of God.'

Stevens scoured Hollywood, and his brain, which was by no means as big of course, to find exactly the right person, and finally after a contract for an enormous amount of money being negotiated by his agent, John Wayne no less, was persuaded to play the role.

On the morning of Wayne's call to the set, excitement reached fever pitch.

Actors in minor cameo parts pretended to be nonchalant over the fact that 'Big Duke', as he is known, would be arriving at any moment to utter his immortal line, and the thousand extras all herded into position for the scene, waited in anticipation. Presumably they also hoped everything would be finished by lunchtime, and they could go home with a full day's pay!

Stevens himself buzzed around the film set, growing agitated at the slightest thing, and actually firing one or two of the noisier extras for talking too loud whilst he was trying to concentrate and prepare his masterpiece shot!

The moment of Wayne's entrance finally arrived, and clad in a Roman centurion costume, carefully designed by the studio wardrobe, he clanked on to the set in full armour, looking a trifle morose. 'Duke' cried Stevens, practically falling at his feet, 'this is going to be the greatest scene in the movie, I am so thrilled that you have agreed to do it for me and I know you are going to be great Duke, only _you_ can deliver this line, out of all the stars in show business, you will give it all the heart-rending pathos it needs.'

Big Duke did not look too convinced about this last statement, but he nodded agreeably and allowed himself to be led to the mark just under the Cross, where the poor actor who was playing Christ, had been hanging uncomfortably for some time, awaiting Wayne's release from the make-up department.

'Now quiet on the set there,' yelled Stevens at the thousand extras, 'I want complete quiet, whilst this very sensitive scene is done. If anyone moves they will be thrown off the set.'

No one dared to bat an eyelid, the cameras were ready to roll, the sound man tremblingly held his boom microphone, and Stevens gripped Wayne's arm.

'Now Duke we'll try a rehearsal, just technical you understand. God you're going to be great, this is the most important scene in the whole movie, and that's why I am so happy we have got _you_, I know you will be fabulous. Now

et's try a little rehearsal? All you have to do is point at the
guy on the cross and say, "Truly, this man was the son of
God." Okay Duke, action.'

Wayne lifted his arm and looking straight at the camera,
drawled in his own inimitable way: 'Truly, this man was
he son of God,' which coming from a cowboy actor, and
not the actual Roman centurion on the day it happened,
hardly set anyone afire with emotion.

Stevens blinked, and then recovered his equilibrium. It
was obviously not what he had envisaged, but he had a
star who was costing him a fortune, so he had to direct him
carefully.

'Great Duke' he beamed as if nothing was wrong,
absolutely fantastic, as I knew it would be. Now we'll try
a take this time, just like you did it before of course? But
er . . . perhaps just a little more awe in the voice? Okay
et's go again.'

The scene was repeated, Wayne looked as if he
understood what was wanted, but read the line exactly as
he had done before.

Stevens' face was a study, but determined to win the day,
he kept control of his emotions and cooed to the Duke
again in a syrupy voice: 'Wonderful, wonderful, that's
exactly what I wanted. Okay this time we'll shoot, and I
want it just like the rehearsal. But please, more awe Duke,
more awe. After all, this guy really is the son of God, and
it's the most important moment in the story. Okay, let's
roll, and remember Duke, more *awe*.'

Wayne waited for the word *action*, and turning to the
Cross, no doubt remembering the colossal wage he was
receiving, and with his director's last pointed instruction
ringing in his ears, did the best he could in true cowboy
fashion.

'Awwwwwwwww . . . truly, this man was
awwwwwwwww . . . the son of God.'

M is for MIMOSA and METHS

Although happily I have no need for stimulants in the form of drinks or drugs, I am not totally sterilised against 'turning on' in certain ways, but my tastes are simple! Not perhaps everybody's cup of tea, so to speak, but there are two very definite things that can make me hit the ceiling, and I do not mean amal nitrate! Mimosa and methylated spirits are my downfall — I hasten to state I do not drink the latter as in the case of an advanced alcoholic, but the mere smell of it drives me mad, apart from its beautiful colour, and if anyone should ever peep through my window and see me sniffing the stuff with such relish they would surely think me crazy enough to certify, and slot me along with glue sniffers who I understand get a big buzz out of this fetish, if that is the right word.

I do not get a buzz out of meths, it's just that I adore the smell, and when the charwoman uses it to clean certain glass objects in my home, the aroma that pervades the rooms for a while fills me with utter delight. Mimosa, of course, is a very different matter and much more normal. There would be no chance of me being described as an addict of some sort if caught sniffing this heavenly blossom, and I am sure I am not the only one who revels in its perfume. I cannot describe what mimosa does to me — it is rather like a nostalgic piece of music in some ways, I suppose. Aside from enjoying its fragrance, it takes me back to Christmases past, when mimosa was always mixed with daffodils, and placed around the winter weary house in order to mingle with the log fires, reminding us that spring was not too far away.

M is for BOB MONKHOUSE

The first time we met was when he and his writing partner, the late Dennis Goodwin, were 'regulars' with me on a radio show entitled *Calling all Forces* which was performed every week from the Garrick Theatre in London. I was twenty and married but I fell madly in love with him. It was not just the way he looked that appealed to me, but his intelligence and wit. To this day I think he is probably the most unappreciated comedian we have here, not to mention an extremely clever and erudite man. Our romance never really got off the ground, which was a shame because at the time I thought we would have made a lovely couple. Nevertheless we have remained good friends — which is a pretty 'milk and water end' description of what I figured then was the Romeo and Juliet affair of the decade. There were times, as the years rolled by, when Bob jokingly used to say that one day when we were very, very old we might finally make it, but by then we would not be able to do anything!

N is for DAVID NIVEN

This debonair gentleman has given us all years of entertainment in films, and recently written two books of the highest and most amusing quality. I have never met him, but we have several mutual friends so I feel as if I know him well, sadly, it has not been my good fortune to be introduced or spend time in his company though. I know I would enjoy doing so for the amusing stories he tells are superb. I came close to meeting him once at the B.B.C. when I was there a couple of years ago, doing a radio play by Terence Rattigan. He was waiting in the corridor to do a show, hosted by disc jockey Pete Murray, on which he advertised his latest book, and I saw him standing outside awaiting his call. For a few moments I suffered the awful inner conflict of whether I should go up and make myself known. In the end I chickened out. I am not a shy person by any means, but I figured what right had I to go and push myself at him, gushing about his books and films. Never mind, one day perhaps?

N is for NYMPHOMANIAC

Unlike alcoholism or drug addiction, little is known of this equally serious problem, and as I am not a man who has had to deal with his wife's insatiable desire for other men, *any* men, then I cannot speak with great feeling or authority on the subject.

I have of course met quite a few nymphomaniacs in my life, and they have always struck me as extremely sad women, desperately anxious to please everyone, man or woman alike, and terrified that some action on their part may hurt or upset another person.

There are too, male nymphomaniacs, but not much is ever said about them for it has always been considered a man's prerogative to chase women, and the more conquests he makes, the more he is revered and admired by his fellow men. A woman on the other hand is merely considered to be a tramp, a slut, or a heartless adulteress, if she is married with children, and this is the way it will always be, no matter how strong a hold Women's Lib manages to gain in the future.

Most nymphomaniacs are not *femme fatales* as one might expect, but often quiet almost mousey little females. Perhaps this is the reason they have strong sexual needs, for I have always maintained that if a woman is greatly desired, then there is no need for her to prove how sexy she is to a man.

The movie sex symbol is, in nine cases out of ten, a quiet, home loving and almost shy woman when it comes to the opposite sex, due to the fact she has to play down her sex appeal. Whereas the actress who portrays a dignified lady, or innocent beauty, must prove to the world that she is basically more sexy than anybody else. Marilyn Monroe had no need to prove herself in the sex department for instance, but one Hollywood actress, famous for her sweet cute roles, along with her Peter Pan collars, which showed no low decolletage, was unquestionably the biggest nymphomaniac in town.

A well bred and shy little mouse who was also married once set out deliberately to take my first husband

Queenie's Castle. (1970)

Dennis Hamilton away from me back in the Fifties. She succeeded in getting him into her bed, which was not difficult in Dennis's case, but when the affair came to light and her husband found out that the faithful creature he had regarded as his wife was really a raving 'nympho' at heart, a quick divorce followed.

At one time I employed a nineteen year old nurse to look after my small son Jason. This girl really looked as though she could have been the local vicar's daughter. She was quiet, polite, and terrified of men, so she told me, due to having been raped by her father at the tender age of thirteen. I was so anxious to protect and help, that I actually ordered all my male friends never to swear in her presence, and asked my husband Alan to be gentle at all times, as I genuinely thought men frightened her!

Imagine my amazement, after she finally left, when I discovered that this virginal and shy maiden had lured most of my friends into her bed whilst I was asleep!

According to popular vote, she was one of the best 'lays' all of them had ever known!

The funniest story I know connected with nymphomaniacs however, did not occur at home, with sex crazed nannies tempting men down darkened hallways at dead of night, but in Leeds where we were filming my successful television series *Queenie's Castle* some years ago.

The director had cast a young actress in the minor role of a nurse (oddly enough) in what was to be a hospital scene where I, Queenie, had been forced to spend a few days.

It was perfectly obvious to all of us that he knew the lady rather more than well, which was probably why she had got the part in the first place. But even *he* could not have realised her sexual appetite was so voracious, until halfway through the week's rehearsals, when it became blindingly clear to all of us that she was indeed a true nymphomaniac! None of the men connected with the show were safe from her advances, but then as she was fairly attractive, they did not seem to mind, and many presumably went the whole way with her!

On the actual day of shooting, I lay in my 'hospital bed' awaiting the commencement of the scene in which she appeared with her 'one line role'. This simply involved wheeling a medical trolley into the ward, and speaking a few words.

The cameras rolled and we went into action. It had been a long, tiring day, and time and tempers were growing short as she trundled her trolley up to my bed, fluffed the lines and blew the whole scene, causing one of the technicians to snap sarcastically, 'That does it. She can now honestly say she's screwed *everything* . . . including her career!'

N is for NAME

'What's in a name?' Shakespeare once said, 'a rose by any other name would smell as sweet.'

MISS DIANA FLUCK and MISS DIANA DORS

In show business, the act of changing one's name is almost automatic. Most stars on the giddy road to fame decide very early on in their careers to assume a title much more glamorous or grandiose than the one they were given at birth.

In my own case, it was not merely vanity, but necessity, to adopt some new and smoother sounding surname, if for no other reason than safety!

To be born with the name of Fluck, particularly if one is a girl, can be nothing less than disastrous. Originally my reason for changing it was no more than a young girl's ambition to become a film star with a beautiful name which would look good in twinkling lights, but when I was cast in my first film the director tried gently to explain that the second part of my name would have to be altered because people might try to place a vulgar intonation on it! I was only fourteen and did not quite understand his well meant reasoning then, but as I wished to call myself something much more exotic anyway, I agreed willingly,

139

and the search for a new surname was on!

My agent had suggested Scarlett, after what had obviously been a wild night out somewhere, and I toyed with that for a while. My own fantasy of Diana Carroll also seemed a possibility, but my father was incensed that the family name was not to be used. 'It was good enough for my father and me,' he raged in my agent's office one day, 'so it should be good enough for *her*.' Happily he was placated on this issue by everyone, and went back sulking to Swindon, for as he was born under the sign of Libra, he hated to be proved wrong over anything!

Finally my mother in a moment of brilliance decided that I *would* stick to a family name after all, and because my grandmother's maiden name had been Dors, she felt it sounded good to have two names with the same initial. So Dors it was and we were all happy!

During my long career I have known many stars, and would-be stars, who have also had to change their names, and it has been very amusing. At L.A.M.D.A. where I studied the finer points of acting, one poor young hopeful in my class was stuck with the name of Janice Onions. Instead of changing her surname as I had done, she unwisely decided to try and alter the pronunciation, and spent the time, instead of concentrating on work, trying to persuade everybody to call her Janice Onigh-ons!

The late musical comedy star Hy Hazell cleverly derived her name from an abbreviation of being labelled Hyacinth Hazel Higginbottom. Dame Anna Neagle would not have sounded half as majestic if she had remained Marjorie Robertson. Boris Karloff could never have seemed so menacing had he stayed as Charles Edward Pratt. Tony Curtis shed Bernie Shwartz which made him sound like a Jewish drug store owner, and Cary Grant transformed himself suavely from comical Archibald Leach. As for John Wayne striding through the dust as Marion Mitchell in all his westerns? I think he would have received more guffaws than Diana Fluck, as Britain's sex symbol, if he had not changed it.

The list of changed names by show business folk would fill a very amusing book, but in the final analysis, one person I feel rather sorry for is singer Val Doonican. Unlike so many stars who drive around in big cars, proudly displaying initials on their number plates like royal badges, he alone can never do so!

O is for ONE-UPMANSHIP

This is a pastime practised mostly in America by comedians, who have to fight very hard in the jungle world of comedy in order to stay 'up front' as the saying goes.

British comedians do not play this game as much, although they too have to fight to attain their comedy crowns, but naturally the competition is not as hard as it is in the States. Comedian Terry Thomas was in Hollywood, and staying at my home in Beverly Hills, whilst taking part in the immensely funny film, *It's a Mad, Mad, Mad, Mad World* in which so many American comics were also appearing it read like a *Who's Who*. Terry was not enjoying himself however, his humour was completely different from his American counterparts, and the rather polite, lazy English pace at which he lived was vastly different from the fast talking, wise-cracking Yanks.

One day after arduous filming he returned home looking despondently exhausted, so I asked him what was the matter. 'You do not seem to be enjoying yourself on this movie' I said. 'Oh God it is awful' he replied, 'I cannot stand the terrible "One-upmanship" that goes on with Mickey Rooney, Jonathan Winters, Milton Berle and the all the rest of them, it's most aggravating.' Not being too well acquainted with 'one-upmanship' I enquired exactly what he meant. He told me it was a continual struggle by each comedian to keep cracking jokes and one-liners all day, as fast as they could reel them off, in order to be first and funniest on the set!

Finally he sank into a chair with a large drink to help him recuperate saying, 'You know Milton Berle has got the best philosophy really. He said today "*Anyone* can be first . . . after *me!*" '

O is for OSCAR

The coveted award sought after by nearly every actor and actress!

Some stars like George C. Scott however, refuse to have anything to do with it, proclaiming loudly that actors should not behave as though they are in a meat market. Unlike most film folk who talk a great deal, but do nothing to back up their beliefs, Scott had the courage of his convictions, and having told the world he would refuse to be there and accept 'Oscar' on the night if he was the winner, did just that! Marlon Brando, already an Oscar holder, believed so fervently in his crusade regarding the American Indians, that he sent a young Red Indian woman to collect his the second time he won.

All this sort of behaviour does tend to put Oscar down somewhat, but whatever certain stars say and do, they can never dim the glory of actually winning it. The late Humphrey Bogart accepted his with delight, although true to tough Bogie tradition, maintained that he couldn't care less about the thing, and used it as a door stop!

Oscar has also the reputation of being something of a jinx to actors' careers, for there are many who have disappeared from sight after receiving theirs, and it is often regarded as the kiss of death to get one.

Actor Paul Newman has been nominated along with Richard Burton more times than either of them care to remember for the award, and each time they have sat in the auditorium on Oscar night, gritting their teeth and biting their nails, but all to no avail. Losing when one is so close must be a harrowing experience and deserves an award for bravery in itself!

It is also interesting to note that both these gentlemen have been married to actresses who were awarded Oscars, namely Joanne Woodward and Elizabeth Taylor. The Newmans' marriage is still going strong at the time of writing, but then Mrs Newman has only received *one* Oscar in her time, whereas the ex Mrs Burton has *two!* Though I am not assuming this is what broke up the marriage, I am convinced that the subject of Oscar winning came up more than once during their arguments!

Despite this, I would, along with many others of my profession, be very pleased to have this problem. Well, it has much more style than arguing about who ran up the enormous telephone bill!

O is for OLDHAM

Not one of the great beauty spots in the world, but home to some people no doubt. It was certainly a pleasurable place for one actor comedian to be when he was on tour in a play, and managed to get a local girl into the back of his car after the show for a bit lof lovemaking.

Finding her responses totally lacking in animation he whispered in her ear: 'Tell me what I am doing to you, go on tell me.' The girl dozily replied favourably enough, but in such a flat Northern accent, it hardly stimulated his ardour, and after more fervent attempts to hot things up, he whispered again: 'Tell me *where* am I doing it to you, *where*.'

'In *Oldham,*' came her unimaginative answer.

P is for PLAZA

There is only one hotel to stay at in New York, and that is the elegant Plaza! I was once advised to move from a lesser establishment where I was booked in and which I did not like, with the words ringing in my ears, 'Go and check in at the Plaza kid, cos that's class.' I hasten to say I was not *that* much of a kid, but in my twenties, still it does seem fairly young, looking back today.

I have had wonderful times there, and many memories flood back to me from the past, some beautiful, some amusing and some rather alarming. I can recall being sent dozens of long-stemmed red roses, and a standing order of one a day with the message 'I love you' accompanying it, by my former husband Dennis Hamilton who was trying to effect a reconciliation, whilst the lover who was the cause of the break-up between us, flew unexpectedly from England and knocked on the door of my suite, hoping to surprise me, or possibly even catch me in a compromising position . . . he did not succeed!

I can also recall another occasion when my door was not merely knocked open, but almost kicked down, by an over zealous Warren Beatty, who could not understand why I did not want to see him at midnight! He was still mystified as to why I had given him the 'brush off' at another time when he pursued me in his car up Rodeo Drive in Hollywood. Poor Warren, I hope you eventually learned that 'you can't win them all'! The most dramatic experience I ever had at the Plaza was during a time in my life when I had fallen out of love with a famous Hollywood actor and we were, I suppose, having our last 'showdown'. After hours of lengthy talk, with his frustration mounting at being unable to persuade me to marry him, he dramatically threw open the window and climbed out onto the ledge some sixteen floors up, threatening to throw himself off if I did not say 'Yes'. Thankfully, I managed to persuade him to come back in, and stop being so melodramatic, and he finally left with tears in his eyes, vowing we would never meet again if he could help it!

When I saw him pick up his Oscar years later, I secretly thought that if I *had* let him jump that memorable night, he would never have been able to go on to such giddy heights, if you will pardon the pun!

P is for POET

The great poet and playright Christopher Marlowe once said: 'Only a poet may dine with lords and sup with cut-throats.' I am no poet, though I have written a good deal of prose for my own enjoyment, and I know what he said is true, for I have done it myself, not once but many times!

144

P is for PARIS

The most overrated city in the world. There is much more FUN going on in Plymouth.

P is for POETRY

There are infinite pieces of poetry and prose which could be quoted here, but to many readers it may mean nothing. Then again some people, including several artistes I know, detest poetry altogether so I will not inflict my own liking for it on anyone who reads this book, save to say that one of the greatest pieces of prose and verse ever written in my opinion, is *The Prophet*, by Kahlil Gibran.

Poetry regarding children has always pulled at my heart strings, more than any other. At the beginning of a film I once made entitled *The Amazing Mr Blunden*, directed by my old friend, actor Lionel Jeffries, whose prowess for

Thanking Lionel Jeffries for the part of Mrs Wickens in 'The Amazing Mrs Blunden'. (1973)

doing films about children is brilliantly unsurpassable (and who, incidentally, loathes poetry) a sad little poem written in the eighteenth century was chanted by boys and girls as they played in the snow.

'Wallflower, wallflower, climbing up so high, all the little children, they are born to die,' saddened and disturbed me, and it was not until I read a chapter from *The Prophet* on the subject of children, that I felt slightly appeased.

Your children are not your children
They are the sons and daughters of life's longing for itself
They come through you, not from you
And though they are with you yet they belong not to you.
You may give them your love but not your thoughts
For they have their own thoughts.
You may house their bodies but not their souls
For their souls dwell in the house of tomorrow, which you cannot visit, not even in your dreams.
You may strive to be like them, but seek not to make them like you.
For life goes not backward nor tarries with yesterday
You are the bows from which your children as living arrows are sent forth.
The archer sees the mark upon the path of the infinite, and he bends you with his might that His arrows may go swift and far
Let your bending in the hands of the archer's hand be for gladness
For even as He loves the arrow that flies, so He loves the bow that is stable.

P is for POMMIES

I have only visited Australia once in my life, but hopefully there is still plenty of time left to go again. For years I fought and struggled against working in the Antipodes, as they did not appeal to me at all, and furthermore I did not think I could bear the accent. However when it became impossible to avoid the journey any longer, I was given the advice that Australians are fine providing one accepts their rough and ready behaviour, and 'tunes out the accent'.

Off I went to a town called Perth, with a heavy heart, imagining it was some sort of sheep shearing station, and wondering if the outside world, as I knew it, would ever see me again!

To my surprise and delight, I found a pleasant part of the world very similar to England, with its beautiful scenery, elegant homes owned by civilised people whose hospitality knew no bounds, and the Indian Ocean providing a spectacular, sparkling background to the whole place.

From this paradise of beauty and beach barbecues, I went on to work in Sydney, which is one of the most swinging cities I have ever known. So much happened during my two month stay there it would be impossible to relate, but I enjoyed it all tremendously, met some fantastic characters and also fell in love, which probably added to the excitement anyway.

The general atmosphere and trends are a strange mixture of America and England, therefore I found it to have the better aspects of both countries. Australians are not too pro-English however.

The British have been referred to as Pommies since the days when we shipped thousands of convicts over there, and judging from the historic records, it is easy to understand why they do not hold us in very high esteem. Australians still nurture terrible stories of cruelty and injustice inflicted on their forefathers, and although they are friendly and hospitable towards the English, when they speak of Pommies, it is usually with a faint tone of bitterness.

As a small insight into their behaviour I will relate a typical story of Australian antagonism towards Queen and country, when Her Majesty was visiting there back in the early Sixties.

147

As she addressed the crowd at one particular gathering somewhere in the outback, the Queen in her usual gracious manner began praising the photographers who had been buzzing around her, attempting to gain exclusive pictures for their various newspapers. 'My husband and I do understand the difficulties which the cameramen have had to endure on this visit to our corner of the British Empire,' she stated, no doubt establishing that despite a certain amount of animosity from those Aussies not enamoured with the English, the country still belonged to us. 'I can honestly understand the problems involved', the Queen went on, 'for I am not unsympathetic to their work. You see my brother-in-law is also a photographer.' Here Her Majesty paused for a moment waiting for the last words to sink in, and possibly hoping they might create a common bond with her subjects.

She may have in fact waited a second too long before continuing her benevolent speech, for a gruff Aussie voice shouted out from somewhere at the back, 'O yeah . . . and *my* brother-in-law is a *Queen*.'

Q is for QUEENIE

I may not be a Queen, but I was once a 'Queenie,' in the television series written for me entitled *Queenie's Castle*. This was a very funny and popular show, and we worked happily on it for a long time until Yorkshire Television decided they had had enough of Queenie and her 'goings on', and brought it to a close. I think somewhere along the way they thought she was giving Yorkshire Television a bad name, but it is not sour grapes that makes me say, I cannot understand producers in charge of our TV entertainment programmes. It seems as soon as they have a successful show they bring it to an end, and start looking around for something else to gamble on.

People still come up in the street begging *me* to bring it back, as if it were in my power to do so, and write letters saying how they wish it would begin again. Children

'All Our Saturdays' — the follow-up series to 'Queenie's Castle'.

particularly loved the character of Queenie, though heaven knows why, as she was always whacking her three sons with a handbag. But sadly Queenie has gone, and I must wait for the next opportunity to arise, whether it is playing a queen, or a commoner!

Q is for QUOTES

I love collecting quotes, in a way it is probably the only hobby I have: Here are a few of my favourites.

'Any woman who reads the marriage contract and still goes through with it, deserves all she gets.' (Isadora Duncan)

'It is just as easy to love a rich man as a poor man.' (Linda Christian)

'America is the only country recorded in history, that has gone from barbarism to decadence, without ever achieving greatness.' (Bertrand Russell)

'He has the air of an irate pink blancmange, wobbling from Lyons Corner House to Claridges saying, No, No, emphatically No, I will not be eaten with a plastic spoon.' (Kenneth Tynan)

'When you see a guy chasing a girl up an alley without his pants, and a knife in his hand, you figure he isn't working for the Red Cross.' (Clint Eastwood, from the film *Dirty Harry*).

'Never mention my name and Frank Sinatra's in the same breath again!' (Lauren Bacall)

'In success unbearable, in defeat . . . unthinkable.' (Winston Churchill on Viscount Montgomery).

'There is nothing more odious for the young, than watching their elders at play.' (Peter Ustinov from the film *The Sundowners*)

'There is no great dark man.' (Quentin Crisp)

'Life is where I am, not some place else.' (Sophia Loren)

'Everything I like is either fattening, intoxicating, or immoral.' (Dorothy Parker)

'I am the best writer in the world . . . there is no more to be said.' (Harold Robbins)

'I just want to sit here and look at him and be happy.' (Francesca Franklyn then four, in love with my son Jason, also aged four)

With Francesca's sweetheart.

R is for PRINCE RAINIER

Monaco's story book prince, who was in his day, one of the most sought after bachelors in the world, with quite a reputation as a playboy!

Before he actually married Hollywood star Grace Kelly, I used to hear some pretty wild tales about his activities with the ladies, and indeed saw a few racy letters he wrote on the subject of the opposite sex to his friend, millionaire property dealer John Gaul, from whom I had once bought a magnificent car with gold fittings.

Many years later Gaul was to hit the headlines in a big way, due to the unsolved murder of one of his wives. But it was a famous film star, and not Gaul, who figured in a rather amusing little story, reputedly true, where the joke appeared to be on the Prince himself!

Some years ago, long after Rainier had settled down to domestic bliss, his colourful bachelor days far behind him, he and an old actor friend were burning the midnight oil together, having consumed a great deal of wine, and feeling happily mellow.

'Tell me,' murmured Rainier drowsily. 'You have led a fantastic life and your reputation with the ladies is famous! Who, in your expert opinion, is the greatest one you have ever made love to?'

'Well old boy,' replied the actor, 'it's frightfully difficult to say. There have been so many, not just in Hollywood, but all over the world.'

'Yes, yes,' urged the Prince, 'but of them all, there must be one who stands out in your mind. Who would it be if you had to choose?'

The actor paused for a while, mulling over the situation, and his affairs with many famous beauties of stage and screen.

Finally, pouring himself another glass of champagne, he drawled without thinking: 'If I had to pick the very best, it would undoubtedly be Graceeeeeeeeee . . . *Allen!!*'

R is for RECOGNITION

This is something which perhaps most people strive for in one way or another, but to those who achieve it, it is a state which does not always bring happiness or satisfaction.

To be instantly recognisable in the world of show-business is the ambition of all performers, some of whom are never really happy unless they are constantly signing their autograph, or posing for pictures at any given opportunity!

Personally I find recognition a setback in many ways, and often long for the luxury of anonymity, but then I suppose I should remember the old adage drilled into most professional folk, 'that the time to worry is when they no longer recognise you or ask for an autograph'.

My old friend, actor and comedian Jon Pertwee has enjoyed fame for many years now, and is always delighted

Recognition was just around the corner for Susan Shaw (15), Petula Clarke (15) and me (16).

to oblige a fan with his autograph. It was therefore something of a surprise one day for Jon whilst walking down a narrow street in Soho, to hear a long low whistle emanating from behind, and a rather gruff voice shouting 'Oi!'

Not imagining that the summons was in any way for him, but probably one of the barrow boys stationed along the street with their fruit and vegetables, he carried on walking until he heard the command of 'Oi' once again, and turned to see who or what it was.

There lolling in a doorway, stood a grimy looking character, who in the days just after the war would no doubt have been described as a 'spiv'!

'Oi' he shouted to Jon, 'is your name Pee-wee'?

'Yes' called the ever amiable Jon, quite prepared for the usual recognition which came his way.

'Come over 'ere,' rudely ordered the oaf in the doorway.

Jon good naturedly did as he was asked, and upon coming face to face with the fellow received the question

'Are you that there Jon Pee-wee what appears on the telly?'
'Yes, I am Jon *Pert*wee,' he answered, stressing the correct pronunciation of his surname, but the cheeky chap ignored his correction pointedly.

'I thought you was that Pee-wee! I've seen you on the telly, and what's more I think you're a prick!'

Totally unprepared for this reception, and ready to sign his autograph in the normal manner, Jon's face reddened as he hastily put his pen away. 'Well I'm sorry you think that,' he mumbled.

'Jon Pee-wee! I knew it was you. You're a prick!' The yob shouted excitedly, now warming up to the situation and becoming quite fierce.

Jon decided his best move was to get away as quickly as possible, and so saying he hastened off down the street, but it was too late for now the wretched man had really got into his stride and proceeded to shout the five letter expletive after him as loudly as he could.

The entire affair shook poor Jon, as it was the first time he had experienced such rude behaviour from one of his public.

Dismayed, and feeling embarrassed by the whole scene, he related the story to his brother, Michael Pertwee, himself a writer of renown, and also a television personality. Michael commiserated with him and tried to laugh the whole incident off as just another crank occurrence, but a week or so later it happened that he too chanced to walk down the very same street that Jon had done on that dreadful day.

Not realising he was doing so, and having forgotten the matter anyway, Michael suddenly heard a long low whistle and a voice calling out 'Oi' in his direction. As he turned around, there was the same fellow leaning against the doorway and making signs for him to cross over.

Drawn rather like a fly into the spider's web, Michael approached and was greeted by the statement, "'Ere, you're Michael Pee-wee, aint you?'

'Yes I am,' he replied cautiously, remembering his brother's experience immediately.

'Yeah I've seen you on the telly too. That Jon Pee-wee is

your brother aint he?'

'He is indeed,' said Michael, wondering what was coming next.

'Well you can tell him from me, he's a prick . . . but you're all right,' he added encouragingly.

'Well if you think I am going to stand here and converse with someone who has insulted my brother, you are very much mistaken.' said Michael loyally, and he walked away.

Unfortunately his actions did not deter the impertinent lout, and the whole street rang to the cries of 'Pee-wee is a prick' until he managed to turn the corner.

R is for DON RICKELS

The American comedian who started the vogue of 'insult' comic, and the funniest man I have ever watched in cabaret.

Nightly, after I had finished doing my show in Las Vegas, Don would convulse his audience, including myself, until five a.m. which was the time his third performance ended at the Sahara Hotel. To me, in that strange twilight world of all night entertainment which every artiste encounters whilst appearing there, Don was a sort of therapeutic delight, and we also became good friends during what was left of the day, for off stage he was even funnier if that was possible.

I have seen him take the biggest stars in show business and not only cut them down to size, but in some cases almost annihilate them, always however with immense humour. Tony Curtis, for instance, one evening became Don's stooge and allowed himself to be dressed as a Red Indian, chanting ridiculous mumbo-jumbo which he had been ordered to speak by the irrepressible Rickels. At the end of it all Don turned to him shouting gleefully, 'Now do you believe you are really an idiot?'

Frank Sinatra too came under fire on many occasions,

and Cary Grant nearly crawled under the table the night he was introduced by him as 'the well known Hollywood fairy!'

Not only show people suffered at his hands of course, he insulted everyone with equal rudeness. One night I saw him actually put a woman in the Ladies' room which was situated very near to the stage, lock the door, and refuse to let her out for the length of his act, despite her threats.

Another night his second show which started at two a.m. went so well, with Don in such scintillating form, that he carried on going, leapt onto a nearby roulette table and began his third show from there.

After a few weeks of this insane entertainment, Don told me that he was going to come to see *my* show. 'Oh no,' I pleaded. 'With your cynical humour, and the way I have seen you behave towards everybody in show business, I couldn't stand it. I would be extremely nervous if I looked down from the stage and saw you sitting there.' '*Never* be nervous,' he announced, more as an order than as consolatory advice, 'no one should ever be nervous in this business.' 'Why do you say that?' I asked. 'Because I had the experience of witnessing Arlene Dahl on her opening night at The Flamingo!' he answered. Still not sure of his meaning I ventured on, 'Was she good?' 'Good?' he stormed, 'She was the worst thing I have ever seen. So if ever you feel nervous before going on stage, just say the immortal words . . . Arlene Dahl.'

R is for GINGER ROGERS

I wrote about Ginger's professional-style tennis playing in my last book, and despite my own detestation of physical exercise, must admit she is a living example of how it can keep you fit, youthful and goodlooking. Ginger could have been a tennis pro. Her limbs are still strong and hard as iron, which for a lady who has reached the maturer years of life, is highly commendable. Naturally, as a child, I watched her dance through countless films with her equally famous partner Fred Astaire. Indeed they were the superstars of the Thirties. She also won an Oscar in the early Forties, and has constantly been busy all through her long and starry career.

But what a horribly fickle business the world of entertainment is. I first met her at the Cannes Film Festival when my film *Yield to the Night* was premiered there as the only British film that year. My star was at its zenith, I was a very 'hot' property, and the press, photographers and fans were having a field day every time I stepped out of the Carlton Hotel. In actual fact it was impossible to walk or move at all. Somehow I would drive through the milling throngs in my powder blue Cadillac convertible, which had been driven over for the festival.

One day we were all invited to the Aga Khan's villa for lunch, and Ginger asked me for a lift back to the Carlton in my car. Naturally I was delighted to drive her and felt rather important to be in charge of such an illustrious passenger, for I was still a fan, having spent so much of my childhood at the cinema. Eventually we arrived at our destination, and there as usual were hundreds of fans thronging outside the hotel waiting to catch a glimpse of film stars, and maybe even get an autograph or two! In order to reach the door it was necessary to drive slowly through the masses. But immediately I was spotted, the scream went up. People began pushing books and bits of paper at me from all sides, and I tried my best to sign them under the difficult circumstances. It was all really like a travelling circus, similar to the way that pop stars are mobbed today. But the thing that embarrassed me most was the fact that not one hysterical fan even offered a bit of paper to Ginger, ignoring her and pushing them all over her head in order to get at me. She took it with great dignity, like the professional actress she is, and when the car came to a halt, slipped unnoticed through the crowds and into the hotel, leaving me to cope with the multitudes.

This brought home a very important lesson to me. I realised that as popular as I was then, there would come a day when I too would be ignored in the rush for some newer star. I hoped that when this happened I would conduct myself with as much dignity as Ginger did.

R is for ROLLS ROYCE

Whatever anyone says for or against this beautiful car, I do not think there is another motor in the world to touch it. In my time I have owned many different types of cars, and among them some very luxurious American ones, but when it comes to elegance and dignity, give me a Rolls every time. When I was married to Dennis Hamilton and very broke, we bought a sleek black Rolls Royce one day on 'hire purchase', and it proved to be our lucky mascot! For at the age of twenty I was the youngest registered owner of such a car in the country. Needless to say this is not the case today, but young or old, I will settle back in a Rolls Royce on any occasion quite happily, and if no-one believes me regarding the merits of this magnificent machine, then ask James Mason's ex-wife Pamela. At the last count she had five . . . all in different colours!

S is for SCOTSMEN

In my last book *For Adults Only*, I was strongly rebuked by many Scotsmen because I had seen fit to ignore their character and sex appeal, concentrating instead on the qualities of others, such as Italians, Welshmen, Frenchmen and even Irishmen!

I would like to now put matters right, by saying that I have nothing whatsoever against Scotsmen, indeed, as a race I find them amongst some of the most attractive men in the world.

If this sounds as though I am trying to toady favour for having previously ignored them in the literary sense, it is not so. My only defence is that sadly and regrettably I have never had a love affair with a Scotsman, and obviously cannot write with great authority on what they have really got under their kilts!

Scotsman picture.

S is for SEX

Sex is wonderful. So much as been written about the thrill, excitement and passion of it all, that to try and elaborate further, even from my position as a deposed sex-symbol, is really quite unnecessary.

However, the outcome of sizzling sex may often be far from ecstatic.

A very beautiful girlfriend of mine who could have been a movie star at least, but settled for the luxury of marrying a millionaire instead, subsequently gave birth to a gorgeous baby and should have lived 'happily ever after' as the story books say.

Sadly the inevitable happened. Due to the lack of servants nowadays, even for millionaires, she suddenly found herself without a nanny.

Obliged to care for the child herself, cope with night feeds and all the other joys which go with being a mother in the early stages, my friend was worn out after only three days.

When I visited her to enquire how things were going, I found an exhausted woman seated in her elegant drawing-room, looking nothing like the glamorous, sexy vision she had formerly been.

Her husband, as husbands do, dozed in a chair, whilst she nursed the baby, surrounded by an array of nappies, bottles and blankets, food stains down the once alluring negligee, and her normally coiffeured hair falling in strands.

Glaring at her man the way women do after the first flush of honeymoon fervour has died down, she observed the entire scene around her and stated dejectedly, 'All this, for five minutes fun!'

S is for SWEARING

I love swearing and I was interested and delighted to read just recently in a medical report that it is considered by doctors to be extremely good for one's health. Letting rip at all the frustrations of life is much healthier than bottling it all up, so they say.

I have met certain ladies who look like shrinking violets, but whose language would make an Army Sergeant Major blush, including one very demure Oscar winning Hollywood actress, who possessed the foulest mouth I have ever heard! My own vocabulary is, to say the least, colourful. I do admit, in the heat of an argument, to using the odd swear word and thereby stressing my point. Actor John Junkin who worked with me on my television series *Queenie's Castle*, did not nickname me 'Leading Stoker Dors' for nothing!

However, I do not swear in front of my small son Jason as I do not really like to hear children doing it, but he has picked up many a swear word himself, and the following incident was therefore very amusing, and typical of his Virgo character. One evening I invited a Catholic priest named Father Simon to dinner. The Father is a great friend of mine, and also the best advertisement for Catholicism that I know, as his views and outlook on life are very modern and updated, and he does not hide behind his Franciscan habit in a world of fantasy, like many other priests do.

Jason had placed himself on the sofa next to Father Simon, who was in the middle of telling us about something that had happened to him regarding one of his parishioners. It was quite a funny tale, and he related it in a very amusing style, at the same time doing his famous impersonation of comedian Eric Morecambe with spectacles on the side of his face. At the end of the story he paused and said, 'I told him not to be so bloody silly.' *'Don't swear!'* commanded my pint-sized son in his best school teacher voice. 'Oh, I'm sorry Jason,' apologised the chastised priest.

S is for SEX SYMBOL

This was a word bestowed upon me right from the start! I cannot find it in the dictionary, and really I am not completely sure what it means, other than an expression describing the effects of the female form on men. No one can define sex appeal, for we all find it in different sorts of people, 'one man's meat is another man's poison', so to speak. An enthusiastic journalist once asked me what I

Marie Windsor and I as two sex symbols — Hollywood, 1956.

thought a sex symbol was. He asked this in the sarcastic manner often used by many of them when interviewing a celebrity. This is usually due to jealousy because the person being interviewed is usually making more money at the end of a week than they do in a year!

Hearing the hiss in his voice and realising that whatever I said would be misquoted and scoffed at, I replied 'Well to tell you the truth, when I first heard the name, I thought it was a musical instrument.'

S is for SMITH

This is the most common of all names throughout the world, but unfortunately 'Smith' has become almost a dirty word in its meaning, due to unmarried people usurping the title, and scribbling it on hotel registers whilst staying together for naughty weekends. If one's name *does* happen to be Smith it can actually be a source of embarrassment when asked to sign some official document or other, as the person concerned appears to be trying to conceal his true identity.

I have known many Smiths in my lifetime, and also had some working for me in the capacity of gardeners, cleaners and nannies, not to mention two hairdressers. At one point there were three Smiths in my employ, which at times caused some confusion, but not half as much trouble as the three 'Mr Smiths' I am about to describe.

Of all the Smiths I have known, three stand out in my mind, whom oddly enough I count among my best friends, not a thing anyone can list lightly. Despite the ordinary sound of their name, *my* three Mr Smiths are totally out of the ordinary, and completely extrovert in their behaviour.

Their Christian names, Edward, Claude and James Marcus, make them all sound fairly dignified, indeed almost aristocratic, but as one was a gypsy, one a pop singer, and one a gold smuggler, this hardly placed them in the select upper crust! Sadly the gypsy, Claude, who was the strongest man I have ever known, passed away with cancer at the age of 35, leaving an emptiness in everyone's hearts who knew and loved him, which will never be healed. Claude was an extraordinary character who had been dragged up in near starvation, by a gypsy mother whose name was Olive Sevenoaks. He was good-looking, elegantly dressed, possessed of a fabulous sense of humour, and as I have already said, the strength of an ox! It is difficult to describe a close friend whose merits mean nothing to those who have not had the pleasure of knowing him, but suffice to say this little epitaph which I write with great sadness, is the least I can do for a friend whom I dearly wish was still here to read this book himself.

The second Mr Smith, Edward by name, who prefers to be called Ben, amongst other things, is a handsome, lovable rogue who hails from the New Forest, and is a constant source of surprise to his very normal parents, being the black sheep of his family, even *before* he became a gold smuggler. His glittering career, if that is how it can be described, came to an abrupt halt when, as I prophesied

163

back in 1967, he would either hit the 'big money' or the 'big house'. He hit the latter and was sentenced to four years in a Chinese jail on an island off Hong Kong named Chi Ma Wan, and his exploits, reported in the British press, showed all the panache of a James Bond. Strangely enough he was introduced to me *by* James Bond, actor Sean Connery, when he brought him along with comedian Bruce Forsyth to my home after playing golf at Wentworth one day, and we have been firm and fond friends ever since. 'Smirker' as my husband Alan nicknamed him, due to the fact that before embarking on something pretty terrible he tends to plant an evil smirk on his face before so doing, would have made a very successful career out of playing golf if he had stayed the course. I do not intend this as a pun, but many professional golfers have stated that he could have been amongst the top ranks if he had settled for golf balls instead of gold bars!

The last Mr Smith, James Marcus alias P. J. Proby, pop star from Houston, Texas, has also carved quite a niche in my life, and for that matter England too since he arrived here in the early Sixties sporting a large bow at the back of his hair. His beautiful singing voice quickly transported him to the top of the charts but his 'hell bent' desire to destroy himself quickly reduced him to the ranks of failure and bankruptcy! Proby's zodiac sign is Scorpio, and as we Scorpios know only too well, the Scorpion stings itself to death rather than give way or admit defeat. Come to think of it we are like the Japanese Kamikaze pilots who hurled their planes at our ships during the war, thus destroying themselves, together with the enemy target! But back to Proby. I met him when he was at his zenith, and making ten thousand pounds a week. Knowing various mutual friends back in Hollywood we hit it off right from the start. I have watched him fall in love with countless women, marrying some, but each affair ended in tears, for like everything he does, Proby acts out all situations to the full. He has a good sense of humour which is probably why we are friends, for I love people who can laugh, but whether or not it is because he is a Texan, he is sometimes apt to be a bit slow on the uptake. He claims to have once attended

Military School in the States, but frankly he does not present much of an advertisement for the place, as aside from anything else his reading and writing leaves a great deal to be desired! This was most apparent on an occasion when he hired the majestic Drury Lane theatre for a 'one man show' come-back, and could neither read or learn the lines of his songs to enable himself to get through it at all, a situation which has probably never been seen on any stage ever before, let alone Drury Lane!

When I first introduced him to Alan before we were married, at a party to celebrate the forthcoming wedding, he eyed him suspiciously, as at the time Alan was wearing a gold earring and discussing the fact that he was of gypsy stock. Proby, like all his other Texan relatives and associates, had a typically Southern outlook on black people, referring to them as 'niggers', and recalling the good old days when he and his Grand Daddy used to sit on the steps of the black porch, shooting 'niggers' up the arse on Saturday nights!

Having listened to Alan discussing gypsies for a while and looking puzzled as to what they were, Proby drew him to one side and asked seriously, 'Just exactly what *is* a gypsy?' He received a lengthy description from Alan, who wound up by saying that like certain other races, they were under-privileged and persecuted people. The Texan mulled this over in his laconic southern mind, and suddenly with a face like thunder demanded, 'Does that mean you are some kind of *nigger*?'

S is for SAGITTARIUS

Sagittarians are lovely people who adore life and exult in large gatherings or company, but woe betide a girl if she gets stuck with one for a husband! Whilst he may thrill and amuse her during courtship, when she finally tries to pin him down in wedlock he will spend most of his time trying to get out of the house and escape! Sagittarians cannot

My own captive Sagittarian.   Terry Thomas

bear to be confined and their heads are constantly in the clouds, aiming arrows at the stars, the archer being the zodiac sign which depicts them.

Sagittarians make good mothers but not necessarily good fathers. Their whole problem maritally is that they are so busy gazing up at the skies, that they neither see, nor care about, the poor unfortunate marriage partners who are being crushed beneath their feet.

T is for TERRY-THOMAS

Thomas Terrence Hoare Stevens, better known as frightfully English comedian Terry-Thomas, has been a friend of mine for nearly thirty years, since I first worked with him on an early television series of his entitled, *How Do You View?* which was then his 'catch' phrase. He is also godfather to my second son Gary, and whenever he was making films in Hollywood years ago, would stay at my home in Beverly Hills, and allow me the same hospitality at his home when I came over to film in England.

Terry would always amuse the members of my staff when they went in with his morning tea. There he would be, sitting up in bed despite the warm Californian climate, wearing a red flannel nightshirt and little red nightcap with the usual tassel dangling on the end of it. At his home in London he had a shield above the bed, sporting his coat of arms and family motto, which depicted the head of a benign looking cow, and the words 'I will not be cowed' written above it. Terry liked a drink when he returned tired from the studio, for he found Hollywood really too fast compared with his somewhat slow, genteel British way of life. This, and the pressures of work perhaps made him drink more than he should have done sometimes, and one night whilst he was staying at my home, and I was away filming somewhere, a rather frightening thing happened.

He had been out to dinner with his agent discussing important business matters, and obviously drunk more champagne than was good for him! Luckily the agent was still reasonably sober at the end of the evening so he was able to drive him back to my house, safely deposit him in the drawing-room, and then wearily return home himself.

An hour or so later he was aroused from slumber by the urgent ringing of his telephone, and upon answering heard a terrified Terry crying down the other end for help. All he could decipher from the garbled chatter were the words, 'Help, I've killed her, her head's come off!' The agent leapt out of bed in a panic, assuring Terry he would rush to him immediately, and this he did, alarmed as to what could possibly have happened. Had his client killed me? No that was not possible as I was abroad; then perhaps one of the maids . . . or maybe a girl friend who had been invited after he left the house?

With a screech of brakes he pulled up in the driveway. Bursting down the front door, he found Terry in tears still sobbing about the severed head and muttering, 'I've killed her.' 'Who, who?' implored the agent in desperation, and then to his relief saw the 'victim'. It was not, thankfully, a human being, but a gold statue of me which stood in the middle of a round velvet seat, holding some flowers. Terry in his inebriated state had fallen over it, and amidst confusion in the darkened room, thought he was responsible for my execution! Upon returning home, I noted that a gold cherub had been discreetly placed where my statue once stood by my embarrassed house guest!

T is for TYCOON

This very word conjures up the picture of a man larger than life, with millions in the bank, and a highly superior brain.

There is not an abundance of tycoons about really, many of the famous are long gone, like Aristotle Onassis, or the great film moguls of yesteryear who built enormous empires in Hollywood and presided over them tyrannically.

In that town, where else? There is an incredibly wealthy business named Forest Lawn, which deals with cashing-in on the sorrows of relatives when their loved ones have passed on, namely a firm of undertakers! Such is the vast richness of this organisation they have turned the grounds of their establishment into a sort of Disneyland, with every kind of souvenir and gimmick imaginable to make money out of those left behind. Huge billboards portraying beautiful scenes advertising the place, are on display all along Sunset Boulevard, rather like the forthcoming publicity of a film. Pink swans glide over crystal clear lakes, amidst soft greenery which welcomes everyone in, both living and dead. Forest Lawn will bury anyone in style, and more than that if the deceased happens to be a tycoon, or someone with immense wealth! At a vast price they will embalm that person, sit him at his office desk, or in surroundings familiar to his life pattern, and allow relations and friends to file past, having their last look, whilst an organ plays suitable music in the background.

With Billy Butlin's son Bobby, David Broome and secret tycoon Eamonn Andrews.

This piece of theatrics is not too often performed however, as there is not a great demand by sorrowing mourners for it. Tycoons appear to make more enemies than friends in their rise to power it seems.

The pleasant and quietly spoken Walt Disney ran his film studios so grimly that it was called 'Donald Dachau's' by the thousands of employees who worked there. Louis B. Mayer was another sincerely loathed by all. He had built the gigantic Metro Goldwyn Mayer Studios from being a poor rag and bone immigrant, and slayed many souls whilst at the top. When he died, the funeral, which was no doubt arranged by Forest Lawn, looked like one of his mammoth musical films, with the church packed full of mourners. 'Alas they only showed up,' remarked a long suffering minion, 'to make sure he was *really* dead.'

Over on this side of the Atlantic we have also had our own tycoons. Sir William Butlin who began life as cheeky and ambitious Billy Butlin, built his fortune on holiday camps, and like Hollywood film bosses, ran them with the same rigid severity as Harry Cohn had done Columbia Studios. Billy was a stickler for work being done efficiently, and the story goes that one day he was inspecting a camp in his usual conservative manner (that is to say he was snooping about checking up on his workers) when he came across two men in dungarees loafing in the sunshine by the swimming pool. White with rage, Billy gave them a dressing down and without giving either a chance to explain, ordered them straight to the front office where he informed them they would be given two weeks pay and sacked on the spot. The men did as they were told, and under the personal supervision of the irate tycoon went to the office and received their money. It was not until after they had left the camp that Billy realised even a financial genius can be wrong. They were not workers after all, but two of his seaside campers! This must have been one of the few times a tycoon did not make a profit out of business!

As Helen in the television production of 'A Taste of Honey'. (1971)

T is for SPENCER TRACY

One of the greatest actors of his day in Hollywood. The wonderful performances he gave in films make Spencer Tracy immortal, and will be enjoyed by generations who were not even born when he was winning Oscars.

It was always my ambition to do a film with him, but sadly this was not to be. However, actress Katharine Hepburn, the big love of his life, did a pretty good job instead, as the movies they made together were fabulous. I did have the pleasure of meeting Tracy once in London when I was sixteen, so at least I am able to add that to my credits. I had been invited to dinner by a producer and his wife at London's Caprice restaurant, in those days the 'in place' for film stars and their like to dine. Naturally I was very excited about meeting the great man. He was courteous, but somewhat quiet during the evening, and as the meal progressed the eight or ten people who sat around him began arguing the pros and cons of acting. As I was so young and just starting my career, I figured wisely that it would be best to remain silent, for one thing I had nothing to talk about regarding film making, having only appeared in a handful by then, and also, I was a little bit shy in such illustrious company.

The argument lasted through the dessert, coffee and liqueurs, with everyone growing excited, and anxious to make their point regarding the subject of acting, but whilst this heated harangue raged on Tracy said not a word.

He sat, head bowed, in the way he always did in films. Indeed most of his work was done that way, especially when he walked from one spot to another, sensitive acting having nothing to do with it, for he was merely looking at the floor to find his chalk mark for the camera!

Finally when the discussion seemed to have exhausted itself, and people were growing tired of the sound of their own voices, an unusual state for show-business folk, my host the film producer turned to Tracy, a trifle surprised that he had not joined in and said, 'Well, what is your opinion on this, Spence? After all you have done more acting than anyone. What do you think about acting as it s today? Should one adopt a method, or take a different attitude?' Tracy remained silent for a moment longer, then slowly raising his head from the depth of the brandy glass where he had been staring, replied 'All you gotta do . . . is learn the goddamn lines!!'

U is for UNDRESSED

There is a saying that 'Clothes maketh man,' and indeed to a great extent it is true. A well dressed person, be it man or woman, may look very attractive with their clothes on, but decidedly not so when stripped and as nature made them!

I read a very interesting article once which said that if men were forced to walk around nude many things would be different, and on thinking about it, it must be right. Wars would be out of the question, for troops could hardly march into battle in their birthday suits; policemen could not uphold law and order, and judges along with other high ranking pompous persons would be cut down to size, thus losing all their dignity.

President Amin, strutting around in the all together is a very comical thought, although it would not seem half as ridiculous as say the Queen riding down the Mall naked!

Everyone is at their most vulnerable without clothes . . .

If a person is caught in the act of unfaithfulness there is very little which may be done except to make some sort of lame excuse, smile, and hope for the best! But if that person is in the nude then it presents even more of a problem as opposed to being muffled from head to foot! I know a few people who have had to try and brazen this situation out, and they have used all kinds of excuses in the process, but one friend did not bother to say anything other than 'So what!' rather cheekily.

This was not the case when an English pop singer I knew years ago decided to accompany me on one of my trips back to Hollywood, and try his luck there in show-business. This was before he had had his first hit in the

Undressed but not uncovered.

charts, and so he was ready and willing to do anything
Whilst socialising all over town, having been introduced to
as many high powered people as possible, he chanced to
meet a very attractive lady one night at a party, and in
short, moved in with her at her apartment in down-town
Los Angeles.

All went well despite the presence of her six year old
child, by a husband whom my friend thought was
divorced and far away, until a certain fateful morning as
he lay in the lady's bedroom, bare as the day he was born!
Suddenly to his horror he heard the sound of what could
only be her husband arriving at the door (husbands only
make one sort of noise and no one needs to be Sherlock
Holmes to detect them). Panicstricken, he dived for cover
in the only cupboard available whilst just like Father Bear
in the fairy tale, having returned from a walk in the woods,
the husband entered growling that he knew Mother Bear
had a man in there. The trouble was my friend did not feel,

174

or look, like Goldilocks as he stood nude and shivering in his hiding-place.

The husband quickly looked around, and on seeing a man's clothing littered everywhere, moved over to the wardrobe and threw open the doors revealing the white-faced pop singer rigidly standing to attention amidst dresses and trappings. 'This is it,' thought he, 'my hour of doom has come, I will be murdered and no one will ever see me again.' This idea seemed extremely probable as the husband who glared at him was at least six feet four inches in height, and built like a tank! As he closed his eyes and waited for fate to strike its last blow, the husband suddenly drawled, 'So that's the way it is, huh?' slammed the door and stalked out never to be seen again.

Whether he returned we will never know, for the would-be British answer to Elvis grabbed his clothes and fled, never allowing himself to be caught undressed in a Brian Rix type farce again!

U is for UPSTAIRS DOWNSTAIRS

As a little girl I used to imagine that one day, when grown up, I would live in a large house with lots of servants to do the work. 'You will need money for that,' my mother warned, but as I had every intention of becoming rich and famous, this problem never caused me any anxiety. How was I to know then that one day the servant situation was going to be a thing of the past, and money the last item with which to tempt anyone to scrub floors, or cook a meal.

Everyone is in the same boat today regarding 'home help', as charwomen now demand to be called, particularly if one resides in an area full of expensive homes, for there is no little old lady who is willing to cycle up the lane and 'do' for a few shillings an hour.

The good old days, as portrayed in the television series *Upstairs Downstairs* are sadly gone, and as one doctor complained to me whilst searching for a part-time gardener to mow his lawn, 'The trouble now is that a prospective employee interviews *you*, not the other way around as it should be.'

Over the years I have had many different types of people working for me in the capacity of housekeepers, cooks, nannies, cleaners and gardeners, and looking back I cannot actually believe that what I am about to write here has really happened, but every word is true!

One of the first housekeepers I had was such an incredible character that it would require a book to describe all her activities, but to condense her slightly, she was a busy-body, a liar, and a nut case, to the extent of ordering meat and groceries on my bill and sending them to her husband in London. This bit of fraud was finally unearthed when a man, who turned out to be a butcher, appeared outside my drawing room window one day waving a chicken. When asked what he was doing by Dennis Hamilton, he explained that he had been delivering the things for six months and never received any money! At this point the housekeeper arrived on the scene looking red faced, so Dennis, who was not known for his patience or placidness, paid the poor man's bill, and threw the bird at her scoring a direct hit! This caused the guilty culprit to slide down the wall wailing, 'Oh, Mr Hamilton, you've winded me on Good Friday!'

At another time when asked why there was inch thick dust on the window sills, she was astounded when I did not accept her theory that they had been cleaned that very morning, 'but a helicopter had gone over and created a 'orrible dust'! Her reign finally ended when, after our departure to Hollywood, she gave an intimate interview on television regarding our personal lives, even describing the way Dennis liked his shirts laundered.

Over in America we did not have too much luck with the servant scene either. Domestics in Hollywood are virtually extinct, and it is left to black people to perform these tasks. This may sound as though they are still working as slaves, but it was certainly not so for our first coloured cook arrived every day in a Cadillac, and

Playing a maid in 'The Calendar'. (1947)

demanded very high wages for her services. Another, who also glided up the driveway in an expensive car, had a fetish about brightly coloured underwear! It was not until I found myself literally without a pair of knickers to my name that I caught her out!

Back home in the so called sanity of England again, I suffered one alcoholic housekeeper who became outraged when I set a trap and found her at the drinks cupboard, topping up bottles she had emptied with water. The next one rebelled about doing a small wash, indignantly snorting, 'I am not a laundry maid, you know'. And yet another who claimed she had once been a society lady, spent all her time showing me old photographs of herself in *The Tatler*!

Having had enough of this nonsense, I applied to an extremely top drawer domestic agency for someone with impeccable references, and subsequently engaged a spinster, who for a while worked well. One day, however, I discovered the Hoover abandoned in the hall, and found

177

she had disappeared with all her luggage, through the window of her room. This behaviour would normally have been written off as just another bizarre domestic whom I had been unfortunate enough to employ, but the woman went straight to a national newspaper and tried to sell her story of 'life with a film star', pretending she had been kept a prisoner, thus necessitating an escape from the bedroom window.

It was quite a long time before I dared engage anyone else after this, as it seemed that employing a servant, in my position, was not only aggravating but downright dangerous! Eventually, I was forced to do so, and the next one in was a German Baroness who had fallen on hard times, though I was assured she held no grudge against the English, and had been trained as a Cordon Bleu cook. Settling back happily, relishing the idea of a feast of superbly cooked dishes, I gradually found out that she could hardly prepare food at all, certainly the meal would always be at least an hour late even if she did. Before I realised that she was so abysmal, I had arranged a rather important dinner party and was surprised when a strange woman appeared at my front door asking for the Baroness. Upon showing her into the kitchen, the woman ran forward crying, 'Oh Madam, whatever are you doing in this awful place?' Not knowing quite how to take this, I retreated back to my guests and waited for dinner, which was then cooked by the Baroness's friend, for it appeared she had once been her housekeeper. This was the only occasion I ever experienced a servant employing her own servant.

After the Baroness's departure, I was persuaded to pay a large sum of money to an agency, on the recommendation of a friend who assured me the only place to get domestic help was from the island of St Helena. My friend was 'gay' and had employed a young St Helenian boy to cook for him, amongst other things. 'The woman you will be getting is his mother,' he stated. 'And as he cooks like a dream, then she *must* be good.'

I waited for the arrival of the lady in pleasurable anticipation, dreaming of a large coloured person, rather ike Scarlett O'Hara's nurse in *Gone With The Wind*, who would prepare delicious food, wearing a scarf over her head and large hoop earrings! My reader can therefore sympathise when I say that the wizened little creature who finally arrived, never having seen an electric stove, was hardly what I had hoped for. On her first morning I tried to explain the workings of the oven, but it obviously terrified the poor woman, and when I suggested she try out a simple bacon and egg meal, which could be done on the electric griddle, she took an egg in her trembling hand and let it go splat on the hotplate shell and all!

Life went on, upstairs and downstairs. I encountered a butler whom I wrote of in my last book and eventually settled in our present home with my husband Alan. With the arrival of my son Jason, I was forced to engage a nurse to look after him. I think she was suffering from the side effects of the Pill which in some cases causes acute depression, as I would awaken in the middle of the night to the sound, not of my newly born baby crying, but her, which did not help anyone to get a good night's rest.

The next nurse worked well for several months, until I discovered that whilst Alan and I had been appearing in the theatre each evening, she was entertaining her boyfriend at our home so generously that she was forced to leave through becoming pregnant. So much for generosity!

Little did I know that the one who followed in her footsteps was going to be much more trouble than a young girl, for whilst her interest in the opposite sex was not, and never had been active as she was a sixty year old spinster, this nanny was a complete lunatic! True she cared for Jason extremely well, but as time went by and he started to grow, she continued to treat him like a baby doll, never permitting him to walk anywhere, so that neighbours thought there might be something wrong with him. She was always smartly dressed, and had a collection of elegantly groomed wigs, due to the fact that she was totally bald; it was a horrific sight if anybody bumped into her on the landing at dead of night, as without hair and teeth she looked as though she had been hired to haunt the place! Her mad reign was finally terminated when the whole house nearly burned down due to her negligence and after the fire engines, and policemen left, so thankfully did she! The new replacement turned out to be an ardent spiritualist, and could be seen walking around the garden talking to trees and blades of grass, not to mention filling Jason's head with frightening stories about spirits and ghosts. Another was so fat, Alan nicknamed her the 'Happy Haystack', swearing that as she ate so much he was convinced one day he would walk in and find her with the refrigerator between two slices of bread! The 'Haystack' was fired after it was discovered she had run up a grocery bill of over a hundred pounds for a month on our credit account whilst we were away, and though she was fat and jolly, I could not afford to keep her at that rate.

Whilst all this was going on inside the house, the situation regarding the outside, namely the garden, was also acutely worrying. A long line of 'tidier-uppers' had been all I could find, one of whom was actually a grave digger, and another who looked and sounded exactly like Michael Crawford. This would have been quite amusing, but for the fact that his work pattern went along the same disastrous lines which Michael encounters in his television series *Some Mothers Do Have 'Em*, so I was obliged to dispense with him.

A Polish gardener was then employed and for a while all went well. I ignored the occasions when he would suddenly rush from whatever he was doing into the rhododendron bushes, and observe them shaking as though blown around in a strong wind. However, it was when Jason filled his lawnmower with water instead of petrol, that the man suffered a complete epileptic fit on the terrace, and left because he could no longer stand the strain of Jason's childish pranks on his nervous system.

By this time we were employing a young redheaded nannie who had quite an effect on the nervous system of the next gardener, due to his peeping at her through various windows in the house. This embarrassed her, and whilst mulling over what we ought to do about this 'peeping tom,' he suddenly decided to run up the lane and stab another gardener in the back one summer afternoon,

Doing it for real, years later.

for reasons which we will never know. The police hauled him away, the nannie left soon after to drive to India in a lorry with a group of hippies, and that was the end of another pair of domestics! A nymphomaniac nanny, as written about earlier, lived with us after this, but she looked virginal, and did her job so well, that we were happily oblivious of what was going on around the bedroom landings at night! The only element of discord was between her and a 'gay' manservant who came to do the housework. He was jealous of her position and strutted around making remarks about 'stupid girls who only wanted to work for film stars because they think it is all glamour, parties, and Robert Redford chasing them up the stairs!' In this case it might have been Redford himself who got chased, but I finally decided to forget the whole miserable business of having servants. This did necessitate hiring the odd babysitter for Jason if Alan and I ever wished to go out for the evening, and the last experience we had finally convinced us that the days of Gordon Jackson as the loyal Hudson, were definitely over for good!

I had found by then an old gardener who was only able to potter around a little, trying to pick up where the one sentenced on a stabbing charge had left off and we thought it would be a good staple idea one evening to have he and his aged wife over to mind Jason whilst we went out. The sweet, old fashioned couple hobbled in, assuring us all would be well after we went. 'You go ahead, Mr Lake,' the gardener said to Alan, 'my wife and I are really grateful to be able to sit in your beautiful home and just watch the colour telly.' Having told them that Jason was already asleep and not likely to spoil their evening's viewing, we indicated they were welcome to make a snack, and cups of tea if they wished, whereupon he bowed us out of the door, touching his forelock saying 'Mr and Mrs Lake, leave everything to me, you are in safe hands tonight.' Away we went, wondering why we had never thought of the idea of inviting them to 'sit' for us before, and enjoyed ourselves to the full, confident that all was well at home. Imagine our astonishment on returning to find both of the dear old souls paralytically drunk, the wife with her legs in the air on the drawing room sofa, and the husband, now falling about, all respect and 'forelock touching' gone. 'Come on in Alan, have a drink with me' he shouted as if it were his home and cocktail cabinet. On surveying the scene we found two bottles of spirits demolished, and the 'snack' we had invited them to make was practically a joint of beef, massacred along with other goodies looted from the larder.

Notwithstanding this the old man, red faced and beaming from the effect of the brandy, gave us one parting thrust before they went, 'Well now' he slurred, his arm around Alan's shoulders, 'we arrived at six, it's now midnight . . . at a pound an hour? Let's call it seven quid and done with it!' Our experiences with servants have made both of us paranoic on the subject, but we now have a gardener working at our home, who is without doubt the best anyone could hope to find. Mario is an Italian, sent to us by a high class villain living in the neighbourhood. This situation recently provoked the local rumour that Alan is no longer an actor, but a member of the Mafia and making money in the extortion racket, thus enabling him to ride about in a smart Rolls Royce! One never knows where ridiculous stories start, but we both felt something more than paranoia recently, when we heard Mario beneath our bedroom window, beheading flowers, and loudly whistling the theme music from *The Godfather*.

V is for VILLAINS

The world of crime has always fascinated me, possibly because actors so often portray villains, and were, a few hundred years ago, regarded as vagabonds and thieves themselves, prohibited from entering many towns at all and having to perform their plays on the outskirts.

I have known dozens of villains in my life and also found them to be completely fascinated by show-business and its personalities. Therefore, despite the titles bestowed upon certain actors and the nonsensical dignity some try to place on our profession, it all goes to show that the two 'occupations', if that is the correct word, seem to go closely together.

The first villain I ever met was the son of a vicar and eventually got himself into a lot of trouble flogging nylons on the black market just after the war. The second is still operating to this day, for although he has been in prison several times, to use his own words, he 'cannot leave the villainy alone.' One fellow I knew became involved in forgery in such a big way that he very nearly upset the entire economy of Switzerland many years ago, and a near neighbour of mine, who to all outward appearances leads a perfectly respectable life, is one of the biggest villains in the underworld, once escaping from a Tangier jail dressed as a nun. If I am appearing to make criminals look exciting that is not my intent, there is nothing clever about spending half of one's life inside, and crime really does not pay, to coin a righteous sounding cliché! Charles Kray, the elder brother of twins Ronnie and Reggie, spent nearly ten years in jail because he was related to them, and therefore 'tarred with the same brush', so to speak. Charlie is one of the most gentle and charming men I have ever met, but even he was enraged when a newspaper reporter, anxious to whip up sensationalism, asked him how he felt about the glamorous life he led. Snapped Charlie, 'I have just spent ten years in prison, there is nothing glamorous about that!' Villains, even to show-business people, do seem to lead playboy style lives however, that is until they are caught! Dennis Stafford, a handsome rogue fitted this picture perfectly even after he had spent a long term in Dartmoor. Upon his release he brought a party of friends, including his father, to celebrate at the club where I was appearing in cabaret in Newcastle-on-Tyne. The champagne corks popped and it was fun and laughter all round until he was sent back inside again, this time for life!

The Great Train Robbers created the most colourful and exciting reputation of all when, having robbed the train in question and made off with two million or so, they were nearly all sent down for thirty years apiece! It was whilst serving his own massive sentence that Tommy Wisbey had to endure the tragic death of his daughter in a road crash, and was not even allowed out under guard to attend her funeral. At the time I felt this was inhuman, no matter what he had done, and sent him a telegram of sympathy. This triggered off a series of letters between Tommy and myself, indeed he also sent me a lovely bouquet of flowers through his wife. My son Jason was only a baby at the time, and one day to my surprise a beautiful teddy bear arrived at the door for him from Tommy. It had been made in prison by a friend of his and was dressed in elegant little clothes, all of course hand made and exquisite. I naturally wrote thanking him for it, and back came his letter saying, 'I am so glad you liked the bear. It was sent some weeks ago, and I was worried in case you had not received it safely. After all . . . trains do sometimes get hijacked, you know!'

An American gangster I had the misfortune to meet once in New York, proudly showed me the scars of his latest battle with fellow mobsters, a paralysed left arm, which he held aloft like a symbol of honour: 'I got this when I stopped five bullets,' he boasted. Another of his associates, with whom a singer friend of mine was hopelessly in love, invited a group of us to his lavish apartment one night and could not resist throwing open the refrigerator door where he pointed to a rather large chicken on one of the shelves. 'See that?' he shouted. 'Stick your hand up its arse.' One of the men in the party did so, somewhat reluctantly, as it was hardly his idea of a thrill, but as it was an order and not a suggestion he did as he was told. To everyone's amazement the bird was stuffed with thousands of dollar bills, just a small part of the loot stolen by our host in some large supermarket hold-up! None of us dared to enquire where he had got the rest of the money hidden, but judging from the puffed up look of conceit on his face it would not have surprised me if he had inserted a few thousand up his own orifice!

V is for VICTOR

This is a tragic tale, but it also has a humorous side, for laughter and tears usually go hand in hand.

Actor Victor Henry was perhaps one of the most brilliant artistes to grace the English theatre, he spoke six languages and possessed something closely akin to genius. For a few short years he went from strength to strength in plays and films, giving beautiful performances which earned him rave notices and awards, but unhappily his weakness for alcohol gradually got the better of him. Slowly his star began to wane, for producers and the like did not wish to employ him often, as his reputation for being a wild man soared through the business like a forest fire.

The sadness of this story, jumping for a moment to his tragic end, is that at the time the lorry mounted the pavement where he was walking, he had been off the drink for many months desperately trying to conquer his alcoholism, and had just completed a television play entitled *Diary of a Madman* in which he ends his days in a mental home, unable to speak or fend for himself. Ironically, and by a cruel twist of fate, this is exactly where Victor is at the time of writing. Instead of killing him, which would have been a mercy, the lorry accident caused serious brain damage, and although his parents and friends all pray he will recover, to date there has been no flicker of life, from the living vegetable who was once actor Victor Henry.

Before fate took such a tragic step, Victor was at the centre of many an amusing situation through his drinking bouts. My husband Alan, his greatest friend, had quite a few adventures and rampages with him when they were working together, and on several occasions I have seen Victor arrive at our front door in the middle of the night, covered in blood with glasses broken, due to some outraged husband taking exception to his philanderings with his wife. His personal life was as big a failure as his professional life had been a success, but then that is often so with artistes. After his marriage failed, he set forth on a succession of love affairs which always ended in disaster, inevitably due to his drinking, for when he was afire with booze he would also tend to become violent with his women and accuse them of anything that sprang to mind!

A particular instance of this happened one evening when he came to our home with some actress whom he had only known for a short while. The night wore on until the early hours of next morning, with Victor drinking his ample quota of brandy, and eventually I decided it was time we all went to bed. Having ensconced the two guests in a room next to ours, I lay awake long after Alan had gone to sleep, for I thought I could hear strange noises emanating from there. They grew louder until I distinctly heard the actress moaning and screaming, and thought in a vaguely amused way that Alan's friend Victor, whom I did not know too well at that point, must obviously be one of the greatest lovers since Casanova!

The cries for help continued, until gradually I became alarmed and nudged Alan to wake up saying, 'You had better go in and see what is the matter, after all he is *your* friend.'

Somewhat reluctantly Alan arose and walked along to their room. Having knocked at their door a couple of times, he entered slowly and the sight that met his eyes was quite horrific. The actress lay stark naked, her undies flung around the room in chaos where they had been torn off, and there was also blood on the sheets. Victor loomed above her like a demented gnome, now ready to pounce on and kill the victim, whose crime he explained drunkenly was actually refusing to say goodnight to him.

Luckily for the lady, Alan had arrived just in time, so having escorted her to another bedroom and given her a shot of brandy with which to calm herself he then issued an ultimatum, 'Right, now we are all going to get some sleep. But if I hear one creak on the landing from either of you, I promise there will be real trouble.' Had I been the actress I would have waited until everyone *was* asleep, and then made my escape! Women are peculiar creatures however and next morning she was still there, suffering more insults at the hands of Victor, who was as usual downing drinks before ten a.m.!

It was while he and Alan were working on a television series together in Manchester, that my caring husband decided it was not safe to leave Victor alone for the weekend, and took him back home to his parents who live in a small village near Stoke-on-Trent. They are kindly folk who have always welcomed any of their son's friends, no matter how bizarre, but Victor was too much for them to take! He had, of course, been drinking on the train journey there, and picked an argument with a man who nearly pummelled him into pulp, so by the time they finally arrived, he was completely blotto and virtually horrified Alan's parents. Eventually, when they had all retired for the night, Alan's mother, who did not trust her house guest at all, and who could blame her, spent most of the night waiting downstairs for fear he might get up to something whilst everyone was asleep. Sure enough her fears were confirmed, when Victor, who merely wanted to go to the bathroom which is situated on the ground floor, staggered out of his room and began to descend the stairs. In a flash, the electric light was switched on by my indomitable mother-in-law who stood like a fire-breathing dragon at the bottom, ready to defend her house and family from any attack by this monster her son had seen fit to bring home. Poor Victor was in no state to harm a rice pudding, and through glazed eyes, hardly knowing where he was, he whimpered that all he needed was the toilet, which was not surprising considering how much liquor he had consumed.

Next day he related the whole story to Alan, saying incredulously, 'What a fantastic electrician your father must be . . . do you know, the moment I placed my foot on the top stair, he had the whole house wired up in such a way, the lights came on automatically!'

V is for VINEGAR

Some people are junkies, alcoholics, pill-heads, 'foodaholics', but I am none of these — my kick is vinegar! I am, to put it bluntly, a 'vinegar addict'. Ever since childhood, due my mother said to her fancy for mint sauce when she was expecting me, I have sneaked into larders to drink vinegar, covered my food with it, and often in restaurants ordered avocado as a first course because of the vinaigrette sauce! Once at a private dinner party, to my delight avocado was served as the first dish. I helped myself liberally to the vinaigrette and began savouring it with such relish I spilt a whole load down the front of my low cut dress. Seeing the liquid gleaming on my prominent cleavage, one of the boggle-eyed male guests, with whom I had been discussing this book earlier, then slyly suggested I entitle it, 'Vinegar on my Bristols'! I toyed with the idea for a while, but the reason I did not settle for that was simple . . . they would never understand what it meant in America!

V is for VIRGO

Luckily I know nothing about the Virgo male on a romantic basis, for if my youngest son Jason is anything to go by, then I have indeed been fortunate! Virgo women are hard-working, industrious, and they also love animals much more than humans, which is probably one of their

Trying to look like a Virgo in 'My Wife's Lodger'. (1952)

most endearing qualities. A Virgo child is super-critical of its parents, finds fault with the slightest thing, and usually much to everyone's annoyance is infuriatingly right! It is humiliating enough to be proved wrong and made to feel small by a child, but imagine the downright shame of having to give in to a Virgo man! Especially if one is a Scorpio like me!

W is for WAXWORKS

It is either very complimentary, or rather dubious, to have one's effigy put into the famous Madame Tussaud's waxworks in London, depending of course on the reason for being displayed there. I always tended to think only of the Chamber of Horrors, when I considered any waxworks, but even the ordinary statues on the floors above the notorious chamber have still, to my mind, a very sinister atmosphere. This is probably because Madame Tussaud herself, who started it all, made casts of the unfortunate people beheaded in France during the Revolution.

I was approached by this famous establishment back in 1957, and considered it rather flattering as to be moulded into wax for posterity is something reserved for only the very famous! I went along and passed through all the different departments, each one meticulously picking out my features, colour of hair, and even displaying a tray of glass eyes to match up against my own.

It was a curious sensation, rather like being embalmed before one's time, but I endured the macabre ritual and in due course a figure of Diana Dors was finished and placed on a pedestal (on one of the *upper* floors I am happy to say), next to such illustrious people in show-business as Sophia Loren, Marilyn Monroe and all the rest who were popular at that time.

It was in my opinion, an appalling wax copy of myself, wearing a rather tatty evening dress which I would never have been caught dead in at a premiere! In fact the whole dummy looked rather like some jaded woman trying to emulate me on a night out!

Years later Alan and I went to a party given by someone with a strange sense of humour, in the Chamber of Horrors, and I took him upstairs during the evening to show him the figure. He was somewhat horrified, as not only did he think it badly done, but in an odd way it seemed to him as if I had actually died.

Regardless of his or my criticism, however, the Beatles chose to put it along with a host of other famous folk on the cover of one of their most successful LPs 'Sergeant Pepper's Lonely Hearts Club Band', and there I am to this day for the benefit of anyone who still has the record, perched at the end of the line next to Shirley Temple, hand on hip, and looking utterly vacuous! There have been other copies of my image roughly done and placed in seaside waxworks like Brighton and Blackpool, plus an incredible life size bust of me, which resides in a fairly new waxworks at Wookey Hole, Somerset. Appropriately this is the place where witches also once lived!

Eventually as my popularity waned in England, Madame Tussaud's decided to melt me down in favour of footballer George Best, and I should imagine, owing to our difference in size, they had quite a bit of wax left over to stick on Mick Jagger as well, with his famous lower lip . . . not, incidentally unlike mine! My last word on the entire subject is about an occasion a few years ago when I appeared within the hallowed halls of Chichester, which I have already dealt with in this book under Jocasta. A sarcastic journalist asked if my future appearance might be with the Royal Shakespeare Company, as there seemed to be no stopping me now! He grinned nastily, and waited for my breathlessly enthusiastic answer . . . 'Why not, I'm already in the waxworks' I replied curtly.

W is for SIR HAROLD WILSON

Firstly let me say I have no interest in politics, or politicians for that matter, although I would like to have met Sir Winston Churchill during his lifetime. Richard Burton once chose to make some very scathing remarks about this great statesman when portraying him in a TV play, and though every public figure is open to criticism and comment, Richard's remarks were extremely distasteful, particularly as Sir Winston had passed on. By the same token Burton received his own 'come-uppance' for doing this, as a riddle about him went round soon after the detrimental statements. 'Why was Richard Burton's father the greatest carpenter in Wales?' 'Because with just one screw, he made the biggest shithouse in the country!' However, this subject is about another eminent politician. Ex-Prime Minister, smart operator, and show-business fan Harold Wilson, now of course comfortably retired and titled after stating at his last election, in order to be reinstated, that he was going to work like hell getting the country together again.

I was not a staunch supporter of Harold during his two reigns of office, unlike a good many of my show-business contemporaries. But it was stupid of me not to climb onto the Wilson bandwagon when it was rolling, like many others did, for now I too might be the possessor of a decoration such as the M.B.E., C.B.E. or O.B.E.

I am all for people being knighted, recognised and thanked for services rendered to the public and general welfare of humanity, but to bestow honours upon actors in my opinion is a joke, for they have done nothing except hack out a livelihood in a fairly easy racket, as Robert Mitchum describes show-business so aptly! In the old days when decorations really meant something, it was an honour, but not today, and when Beatle John Lennon sent his M.B.E. back I was the first to applaud his courage. I do not mean I approved of any rudeness he showed towards the crown, but at least he stood by his own convictions.

During Harold Wilson's reign as Prime Minister, aided by the domineering Lady Falkender (note they bestowed titles on themselves, despite the fact that as Socialists everyone is supposed to be on the same level), many show-business folk were awarded decorations. Apart from Lady Falkender's obsession with the theatre, there was also an actor who became great friends with Sir Harold, to such a degree that he would spend weekends at 'Chequers', advising him on certain matters, and keeping him laughing as in the old days of the Court Jester with the King. It was he who helped start the much publicised and criticised cocktail parties at Number 10. These became such an everyday occurrence, with show-business people merely dropping in at odd times for drinks, that newspapers began commenting and lampooning the situation, to such an extent, things had to be calmed down.

Whilst all this partying and gaiety was going on, actors, actresses, disc jockeys and singers, were having M.B.E.s and O.B.E.s dished out for their services to show-business like jelly beans, thus making a mockery of something which had once been a distinction of honour and respect. One actor, before being actually knighted, declared that any one who was *not* a Socialist merited nothing. He then commenced to sell his house at an enormous profit, but never shared the proceeds with his political party, or even donated some of it to charity, which presumably is what Socialism is all about!

When I look back at the Wilson regime now, and read revelations of the 'goings on' at Number 10, the titles bestowed upon all and sundry, and the sudden retirement decision taken by Sir Harold at a disastrous moment in our history, it gives me terrible forebodings about politics and the men who run our country. My last word on the subject, for the moment anyway, concerned a time in 1965 when the Socialists led by *Mr* Harold Wilson were elected into office, and an actor friend whose politics were extremely Left Wing, decided to send a congratulatory telegram to him whilst staying at my home for the weekend. I did not know about it at the time, but when he revealed what he had done later, I angrily gasped 'How dare you send it on *my* phone'. He made no offer to pay for it of course, but then with his political outlook I suppose he thought we should all live in a sort of commune! The telegram did not ingratiate him however, for he was never among the lucky ones to receive a decoration, but he did manage to get an invitation to

Number 10 one afternoon for tea. This turned out to be a somewhat boring experience, as it was around the time of the first Rhodesian crisis, and Mrs Wilson spent most of the tea-hour complaining bitterly about Ian Smith's treatment of 'her Harold', down the unlucky actor's earhole.

W is for WRIT-SERVERS

This is a strange occupation for a man to follow, certainly not a very rewarding one, and sometimes downright dangerous, as in the case of the server ordered to give a writ once to my old friend, film actor Victor Mature. Having waited around for a day and night outside his plush rented house in Curzon Street, Mayfair, which was actually the subject of the legal matter owing to all the noise Vic was making with his wild parties, the poor man finally managed to pounce on him when he was leaving for the film studios one morning at six a.m., only to be kicked up the behind into a gutter by one of Vic's henchmen!

Writ-servers make a habit of surprising their victims, which is probably the only sure way they know of serving them in the first place, but to play the 'writ game', as I came to know it, takes quite a lot of experience on the part of the person being hunted. I have, over the years, learned to cope with avoiding these wretched men, who always apologise for carrying out their 'duty', as they describe it, with the air of an executioner who is about to lop off one's head!

In the old days when I was being chased by the Inland Revenue for taxes, and it became apparent to them that they had to make me bankrupt, I successfully dodged the various writ-servers who came poking around my house, for nearly two years! In the end I began to tire of the game, and finally capitulated out of boredom more than anything else, but it was great fun while it lasted.

One rather ancient server accosted me at my front door and did not recognise me immediately, due to the fact that

Immediately before receiving a writ.

I was in my dressing-gown and devoid of make-up that morning. I informed him that Miss Dors was away and left it at that, but imagine my surprise when five minutes later he came snooping around through the back garden, and in by the french windows. 'Are you sure you are not her?' he enquired suspiciously, peering at me from under his thick glasses. 'You do look a bit similar.' 'Yes, I have often been told that,' I replied quickly, 'but actually, I am a cousin who is merely looking after the house in her absence.' This seemed to placate him and so off he went. Another one walked down the driveway with me once, discussing the face that he would have to come again when the *real* Miss Dors came back from her holidays (which was where I told him I had gone). All this kind of behaviour led me to believe that writ-servers are obviously not hired for their great intelligence or common sense, despite the popular belief which they too seem to share, that they are a wily bunch who can track down anyone!

On the day I decided to let them *win* the writ game, I arrived home and found amongst other people in my house, the local vet, who was well known for his love of the bottle. It seems that someone had also let the writ-server into the house, and there he had been for an hour or more, sitting comfortably on the drawing room sofa exchanging stories with the vet, and both getting well sozzled on my brandy in the process.

The vet rushed into the kitchen as soon as he knew I was back, and proceeded to play the entire scene as if it was straight from MI5. 'Now you creep upstairs' he slobbered, 'and I'll hold him at bay for a while longer. Leave it to me, I'm used to this sort of thing.' I quickly imagined that with his track record of drunken driving and general lack of finances, he no doubt knew what he was talking about, but having had two years of this cloak and dagger stuff, I made up my mind then and there to bring it all to an end, and assured the worried vet all would be well if he would allow me to deal with the matter myself. So saying, he rushed back to the cocktail cabinet for two more large drinks, and I am convinced to this day that no other writ-server has ever been treated so hospitably.

The most spectacular piece of writ-serving I endured, and one which certainly paid me back for all the trouble I had given the law, was a time when I had been invited to a big film premiere in the West End, and duly arrived in all my glory at the theatre. As I stepped out of the limousine, with flash-bulbs popping, a man ran out of the crowd and literally shoved a large piece of paper in my hand, which naturally the Press photographed immediately.

I did not really know what had happened until I got inside and opened it, only to find not, as I thought, a request for an autograph, but a writ! The writ-servers had triumphed over me for the first time, and running true to form taken me by complete surprise.

X is for X

There is very little I can write under this letter, as X, like Certificate X, or the anonymous Madame X in court cases, must always be censored and secretive.

X also sounds something like Sex and is usually synonymous with that subject anyway, therefore whilst I could write many sizzling things, they would hurt a great many famous people and this is certainly not my desire. In order to complete this piece however, I will adopt the methods of gossip columnists in Hollywood, and various scandal magazines all over the world, by merely asking a few titillating riddles, and let everyone try to unravel them for themselves! For instance which two Oscar winning stars, one black, gave their studios a headache trying to keep the big romance quiet, because they feared it would endanger their box office popularity in America?

Why did Frank Sinatra become so angry and throw Lana Turner out of his house in Palm Springs, when he returned home unexpectedly to his wife, Ava Gardner?

Who was the sweet little English singing star caught by her son's nanny, literally in the act with a girl friend, and a Mars bar?

Which two Hollywood stars ran away to Mexico together after working on a film, but were brought home, reluctantly, by their respective spouses because the man had unfortunately caught chicken pox en route?

Who was the young actress whose mother telephoned me early in the morning to give her a change of studio call

One of my X-films, 'The Weak and The Wicked' with Glynis Johns.

quite casually, knowing she had spent the night on a rug in front of my drawing room fire with her new singer boyfriend?

What was the name of the now retired show business columnist, married to a television comedy actress, who pretended to be actor John Mills and got all the girls to perform under a two-way mirror?

Which American comedian, who has publicly maintained a faithful, happy marriage for a quarter of a century at least, keeps his mistress in a luxury home up in the Hollywood hills?

Who was the sugar sweet singer and film actress, who disinherited her father for marrying a coloured woman, and then bought a house next door to mine in Hollywood for her black boyfriend?

And lastly, a riddle I am still trying to work out myself! . . . Danny La Rue once told me that actor Paul Newman was not very liberally endowed in the lower region . . . I wonder how he knew?

Y is for TOMMY YEARDYE

This affair I choose to describe as my 'muscleman era'. I suppose everyone goes through a strange time in their lives when they fancy certain individuals — only to look back and wonder what the attraction was. I met Tommy, who was a strikingly handsome, tall, dark lad of Irish origin, on the set of a film I made with Victor Mature. He was an aspiring actor, who had also done stunt work for Rock Hudson in his time, and was then doing the same for Mature. Tommy, in spite of his rugged build, turned out to be a very gentle person, and from the moment I looked into his green eyes, I was a 'goner'! My marriage to Dennis had reached a bad stage; it was six years old and I wanted out anyway, as I had had enough of being dominated and manoeuvred. At twenty-five years of age I seemed to have been married all my life, yet never lived, so it was only natural that I wanted a little fun. I was also afraid of Dennis and his violent rages, so Tommy to me, apart from being attractive, was like a strong oak tree against which I could lean and catch my breath after the tumultuous years of living with Dennis. In short we started to have an affair, and Dennis subsequently found out about it. The grand climax came one day after Dennis left our penthouse home on the river at Maidenhead, and we had mutually agreed to part. Singer Shani Wallis, and a male friend, Tommy and myself, went out for a drive, arriving back at the house to find Dennis there in a blazing fury. He lured me inside on some pretext, and then insisted I sign over to him *everything* I owned — cash, cars, clubs, property, a boat, even camera equipment, whilst Tommy and the others waited outside in the car. Having got what he wanted, he began punching me in the head, and breaking my eardrum amongst other things. Tommy saw through the window what was happening, raced to my aid like Sir Galahad, and overpowered Dennis probably for the first time in his life, as no one had ever dared do such a thing before. We left, and Tommy took me to his mother's home in Hendon where I moved in for two weeks whilst sorting things out before going back to my penthouse again.

Dennis, having been the recipient of Tommy's muscle, kept well away from it, but it was a bizarre situation — Tommy and I living in the penthouse, and Dennis living next door in a sumptuous block of flats which I once owned (and which twenty years later changed hands for three million pounds — oh the folly of my ill-spent youth!). Dennis then embarked on a 'one-upmanship' lifestyle, to try and outdo everything we did, his philosophy being that if his marriage had failed then everyone else's was going to do so as well. He set out to break up as many as he could, resulting in three women trying to commit suicide right there in the block of flats. Nightly, taxi loads of girls would arrive at his flat, and as we were having quite a few parties too, this particular reach of the quiet River Thames became almost as lively as the Edwardian days when King Edward VII made Skindles Hotel and Maidenhead pretty notorious himself!

After a year or so things reached a pitch where I wanted to get away. There had been a nasty business when someone who had fallen foul of Dennis, set fire to and destroyed his beautiful river boat, so naturally we were the first to be blamed. Retaliations started — like burglaries, and bricks being thrown through my dining room window. Dennis even threatened to take us to court, bribing actors who were out of work to say they had actually seen us go on the boat and set it on fire. It was plain that life was getting to be too much under those circumstances, so I bought a beautiful fifteenth century farm in Sussex, and as all Tommy had ever done since our association was pick up bar bells with which to do his weight lifting exercises, I thought it would be a good idea, for he always boasted to me that if we lived on a farm, then I would *really* be able to see what he was capable of doing! We moved there and over a period of one year, the only thing I ever saw him do, other than his exercises, or lying in a garden chair acquiring a sun tan, was paint the barn door! It was probably the first nail in the coffin of our relationship, because although he was sweet, he did not possess a very high intellect, and had become rather boring. A Hollywood producer once said to me during my first stay there, 'When you finally fall out of bed, you've got to have something to talk about.' I was beginning to find out that he was right!

To move on as rapidly as possible in the Yeardye saga, we now jump to a nightclub in London called 'The Stork Room' where one night we saw a young comedian named Dickie Dawson performing, and were highly impressed. So much so that when I signed a contract to take the Diana Dors Show on tour, and we needed a comedian, Tommy insisted we should engage Dawson. This was of course the worst mistake he ever made, for the world now knows that Mr Dawson and I not only fell in love, but married eight months later, after Dennis's tragic death, and had two beautiful sons as a result. Dickie was everything that Tommy was not, and as I have always been such a sucker for humour, it was little wonder that I went for him after the boredom of Tommy.

My romance with Dickie blossomed, and Tommy went back on the farm. They say 'Hell hath no fury like a woman scorned', but I was to be a living example of how the tables can be turned the other way.

During our relationship, in order to avoid Dennis getting at any of my money, I placed £12,000 in a safe deposit box at Harrods, to which Tommy also had access. He intimated that he would get even with me for jilting him on the telephone one day and that I would find out how when I returned from the tour. I forgot the conversation and assumed he was merely being spiteful, but to my dismay when eventually opening my deposit box, I found he had removed every penny of the £12,000! Furthermore, there was no way I could prove what had been in there. I called his mother who was naturally upset that I should accuse her son of stealing the money, and refused to tell me of his whereabouts. All our mutual friends pretended ignorance, despite my pleadings that I would *have* to go to the police if he did not bring it back. Several frustrating days went by, and finally I had no choice but to report the whole matter at Chelsea police station. The police promised to do all they could, but it was not until a few days later quite by chance that a friend rang to say his wife, who was holidaying in the South of France, had seen Tommy lying on the beach at Cannes in front of the Martinez Hotel where he was staying. Things moved very quickly after this, the police cast their net, and Tommy, who did not wish any trouble, hastily flew back to England in a blaze of publicity, openly stating he had just meant to frighten me and would repay every penny.

For a year Tommy revelled under the title of Diana Dors' ex-boyfriend, both in the press and socially, but I knew it was only a matter of time before the excitement went stale. He is, at the time of writing, a very rich man, with two Rolls Royces and a yacht in the South of France! I do not bear him any grudge, why should I? Thankfully he has made a success of his life, for there was not much future in 'falling off horses in films!' as his mother once so aptly put it.

Y is for YORKSHIRE

The statement I made in my last book about this beautiful county being 'the best place to lose one's virginity,' brought forth a violent reaction from its inhabitants. For a start no one was quite sure whether to take it as a compliment or not, Yorkshire minds being somewhat suspicious about outsiders discussing their beloved birthplace, but the real furore was over whether I was speaking personally from experience on the subject!

From the moment I set foot in Yorkshire to promote my book with signing sessions, Press and television interviews, etc. the question about the loss of my virginity, where, when and how? became an all important issue. Things really reached fever pitch when the dignified 'Yorkshire Post' ran the whole matter as a headline, and it became the topic and general game for all to discuss and play for several days.

Naturally I parried sly questions from reporters as well as I could, but on a big local T.V. show it was not so easy, due to the fact that the interviewer had obviously worked himself up into a froth about meeting me in the first place. No doubt he recalled, as so many men seem to do, his adolescent years and sexual awakenings, which from the look in his eyes started with a few of my old pin-up pictures! Finally he could control himself no longer and with a leer spreading over his face, and sweating profusely, he asked point blank if I had actually done what he thought I had done out there on the Yorkshire moors? I did not tell him any more than I am telling now, but for those who are still interested . . . I think if you are determined to lose your virginity, what better place is there to do so than the beautiful rolling country of the Ridings?

Y is for JESS YATES

It is not often I revel in someone else's misfortune, but in the case of the 'Bishop', as he was commonly known inside show-business, I did just this.

Each week as he sat at his organ, the musical kind, simpering about Christianity, hoodwinking millions of viewers into thinking he was holier than holy, I hoped it would merely be a matter of time before he was deflated, and it took my old friend Hughie Green to do it. Hughie has had many critics in his life, and he knows what it feels like to have his nose rubbed in the dirt, but after a serious row with Jess Yates all his power was put into top gear and the inside story was revealed, of the man millions thought was cleaner and more untouchable than Elliot Ness.

Happily I never met him during his reign, but I did put out a feeler once that I would like to appear on Stars on Sunday and was firmly turned down by a minion, obviously speaking on his behalf. In so many words the idea of Diana Dors daring to think she could be on the Bishop's hallowed show was unthinkable; with my scarlet background there was no place for me on Christian territory! Jesus had forgiven Mary Magdalene, but there was no way that Jess Yates was going to forgive me! . . .

Two reasons why Jess Yates turned me down.

and yet in retrospect who the hell was *he* to forgive anyway?

Another Diana also suffered the arrows of the Bishop's wrath, namely Diana Rigg who actually dared to suggest that she too appear on the show, but horror of horrors, although her publicity track record was nowhere as bad as mine, she was at the time committing the cardinal sin of 'living with a man' with whom she was in love, and this did not measure up to the Bishop's pattern of decent Christian behaviour.

Weekly I would see show-business people with much worse private lives than Diana Rigg, or myself, smarming and pontificating their way through this immensely popular show, together with Jess himself, and it made me angry that the public were being played for idiots. The rows of virginal maidens who looked as though 'butter wouldn't melt in their mouths', had mostly been personally vetted by the Bishop, and as long as his success lasted, there he leered with the strains of 'Ave Maria' softly playing in the background.

When he was finally dethroned, defrocked and the truth about his own personal life revealed in the newspapers, my theory regarding hypocrites was cemented, and even my mother-in-law who seemed to like him, along with all the others, was forced to admit that I was right after all. At the time I was appearing in cabaret, and during my act asked the audience if there was *anything* they would like to find out about me that they did not already know. A little old lady sitting at the back called out in her North country accent, 'Ee, Diana, why don't you tell us some real scandal.' The answer I gave received thunderous applause and laughter. 'My darling, if I did that, I'd make Jess Yates look like Noddy in Playland' I retorted.

Z is for DONALD ZEC

In my opinion the wittiest show-business journalist we have in this country! I met Donald nearly thirty years ago, when we were both starting out in our various fields, and have followed his marvellous columns ever since, always finding his style of writing hilarious, even when it was against myself.

In 1957 when the television show 'This is your Life' had me as its victim, Donald was brought on to give an acid speech to start the ball rolling. Along with all the other cooing which is prevalent in this show, it made a bit of excitement and truth for a change, and even though I probably cringed at some of his merciless criticisms, I had to admit he was right.

In my life I have received as much publicity as Errol Flynn though I never paid for it, and my name and photograph have appeared in thousands of newspapers all over the world. Of all the publicity I have received, good, bad or otherwise, none has been so fantastic as the time when Donald Zec allotted me three whole pages of the Daily Mirror — front cover and two inside pages, with the heading 'Blond Gold Mine' to titillate the readers! He also titled me 'The Bosom of Bray' when I lived there, which provoked much mirth, and after I bought a fifteenth-century farm in Sussex, he changed it to the 'Bust of Billingshurst'. His descriptions of my opulent style of living back in the early Fifties caused such a furore that the income-tax man came around personally to investigate the tiger-skin rugs which he had vividly described, and my earnings were even discussed on the lunch-time news, thanks to Donald's handiwork.

Yes Mr Zec, I have a great deal to thank you for, one way and another. I still respect your pen, whether it is dipped in sugar or spice, and if I were unable to write a book myself, I can think of no one I would rather have do it for me.

Z is for ZEN BUDDHISM

I know absolutely nothing about this religion, but after asking a friend who studied it slightly at one point in his life, I found out in order to write this piece, that it is a further form of Buddhism which goes beyond the worship of Buddha, or God, and embraces the belief that everyone must literally 'do their own thing'. In short, if you ask a Zen Buddhist whether there *is* such a person as God, or if there is a life after death, he will probably tell you to go and ask the door, or even chop it down, instead of asking foolish questions which mere mortals cannot answer!

As my reader can see, I know even less about it all now than before I tried to glean information, but actor Keith Michell is a keen follower of this cult and it seems quite obvious to me that he went off and 'did his own thing' by embarking on a macrobiotic diet either for his health, or religious reasons.

I was struck noticeably by his loss of weight as a result of this diet and asked how quickly I could do the same, but when he told me that all he was allowed to eat were a few strawberries and some special rice, washed down with water, I drew back in alarm. I have not the willpower to stay on an ordinary diet, let alone one which starves the body, although Keith assured me it cleanses and stimulates the brain whilst so doing.

Actress Diana Rigg, probably still reeling from Jess Yates's rebuff, was also fascinated by Keith's diet and religion. Whilst working with him in a play, and one night after the show, he invited her, together with actor Timothy West, to dine with him and his wife at a special macrobiotic restaurant in London. Off they went, hungry as hunters, and waited for Keith to order for them, as naturally they were new to the whole scene! Eventually some sort of concoction was served with glasses of water placed discreetly alongside their plates, and when Diana tentatively inquired if they might possibly 'lash out' by having a small bottle of wine, she was frowned on heavily by her host.

As Keith and his wife munched away contentedly on their rice, Diana and Timothy, becoming more ravenous by the minute, devised a plan to make their escape, pretending something about an important telephone call coming from New York, they both muttered their thanks for an enlightening meal (no pun intended) and made a fast getaway!

'God, Buddha, or whoever, *I must eat*' said Diana, and seeing a steak house nearby, they rushed inside and ordered a slap-up dinner with all the trimmings! Having devoured it, and in the act of contentedly licking crumbs from their lips, Timothy chanced to look through the window where he perceived Keith and his wife strolling by, no doubt walking off their macrobiotic repast. 'Christ,' he shouted, 'they'll see us for sure.' 'Under the table!' ordered Diana, a lady never at a loss for words in any situation, and so saying they frantically dived for cover below the salt! Happily they were not espied by their Zen Buddhist host, and to this day Keith is probably nursing the idea that he helped guide two more human beings towards a healthier and more religious life.

Z is for ZODIAC

During this book, and in *For Adults Only*, I have referred briefly to certain signs of the Zodiac which usually interest people, for even the most cynical amongst them are well aware of their own birth dates, and not averse to perhaps reading their horoscopes in the daily newspapers.

I like to think that my observations regarding the behaviour of folk born under various signs is fairly accurate, but I cannot generalise and am only speaking from my own experience!

As the last piece in this book, I think it appropriate for me to list what I consider to be the most significant factors regarding *men* under the twelve signs of the Zodiac . . . I would never presume to calculate women on such a sweeping basis!

Capricorn	Impossible, irresistible, but watch them!
Aquarius	Sensitive, exciting but they'll break your heart!
Pisces	Deep as the ocean, fun, but be careful!
Aries	Forthright, strong, but not to be trusted!
Taurus	Romantic, passionate, but never turn your back!
Gemini	Amusing, adventurous, but infuriating!
Cancer	Bright, comfortable, but very possessive!
Leo	Magnificent, reliable, but they also bite!
Virgo	Methodical, artistic, but how they criticise!
Libra	Beautiful, poetic, but God help you if ever wrong!
Scorpio	Sexy, magnetic, but *lethal!*
Sagittarius	Breathtaking, dreamy, but never try to pin them down!

Of course these descriptions may not fit your man, but they could save some poor single females from disaster in the future. You have been warned!